WOMEN'S VOICES
AND THE
PRACTICE OF PREACHING

Women's Voices
and the
Practice of Preaching

Nancy Lammers Gross

WILLIAM B. EERDMANS PUBLISHING COMPANY

GRAND RAPIDS, MICHIGAN

Wm. B. Eerdmans Publishing Co.
2140 Oak Industrial Drive NE, Grand Rapids, Michigan 49505
www.eerdmans.com

26 25 24 23 22 21 20 19 18 17   1 2 3 4 5 6 7 8 9 10

ISBN 978-0-8028-7322-4

Library of Congress Cataloging-in-Publication Data

Names: Gross, Nancy Lammers, 1956–   author.
Title: Women's voices and the practice of preaching / Nancy Lammers Gross.
Description: Grand Rapids : Eerdmans Publishing Co., 2017. |
    Includes bibliographical references and index.
Identifiers: LCCN 2017006749 | ISBN 9780802873224 (pbk. : alk. paper)
Subjects: LCSH: Preaching. | Women clergy.
Classification: LCC BV 4211.3 .G76 2017 | DDC 251.0082—dc23
    LC record available at https://lccn.loc.gov/2017006749

To Anna and Abby

Contents

Foreword

I had always imagined that the first time I tried on the ministerial preaching role I would be in a tall pulpit, six feet above contradiction, looking down at eager, biblically literate listeners desperate for my next exegetical move. Instead I was in a mental hospital, preaching my first sermon across a conference table to five patients who thought they had signed up for a group session on spirituality with a beloved and experienced chaplain. They were about to be treated instead to a scholarly lecture on Galatians that I mistakenly thought was a sermon. That first effort was interrupted repeatedly by a woman who demanded that we pray to Princess Grace.

"You can pray *for* Princess Grace and other heads of state," I explained, "but not *to* her, because that would be crazy." I could tell by their expressions that they had not come to the chaplain's group to hear yet another person call them crazy, so I corrected myself by saying, "Not that I'm calling you guys crazy in a bad way or anything. I mean, yes, you are in the psych unit of course, but who am I to judge?" They glared at me long enough that my voice trailed off into mumbling, which was the sign that I might as well start reading my prepared sermon, complete with theological block quotes and footnotes.

And read it I did. I read it in the voice of the teachers I most ad-

Lillian Daniel is the author of *Tired of Apologizing for a Church I Don't Belong To.* She is an occasional teacher of preaching and a constant practitioner. You can hear her on Sundays at First Congregational Church in Dubuque, Iowa.

mired in Divinity School, which is to say that I had practiced eliminating every trace of personal passion from my delivery. I was convinced that a plain and monotonous style would lift me up in the patients' intellectual estimation, to the level of the cold, dispassionate academics whom everyone listened to.

Context is everything. Yes, as a grad student, that was who I listened to, but these patients were not interested in the role I was trying to inhabit. They snickered, giggled, interrupted, and rolled their eyes as my voice became colder and then softer and it was as if I was talking to no one in particular but I continued mumbling nonetheless, for this was how smart people talked. If you were smart, people listened to you, so I wanted to sound smart. But despite my best efforts, no one seemed to think I was smart or worth listening to.

As the weeks progressed, I became convinced that there were two reasons none of the patients paid attention to anything I said. The first was that I wasn't allowed to wear a clerical collar and the second was that they were mentally ill, the implication being that every sane person would be eager to hear from me, if only I had the visible sign of clergy authority around my neck.

"Here's what I think would happen," my chaplain supervisor told me when I wondered out loud about how a collar like hers would change the way I was heard on the ward. "All those people you want to respect you … they'd just look at you in your collar and say 'Who's that little girl and why is she running around the psych ward wearing a clerical collar?'"

At that point, I added a third reason to my list of why I wasn't being listened to. They were sexist. Not just the patients but the female chaplain too, whose age I estimated to be somewhere between forty and one hundred—in other words, she was too ancient to understand. Didn't they know how hard it was to be a young 5′ 1″ petite blonde divinity student without a clerical collar in the age when second-career men were the darlings of the mainline ministry?

Looking back, I now see that I was vaguely right in my reasons, but I had them all reversed. The patients' primary barrier to listening was indeed their mental illness. But as to who was delusional, it was me on the subject of clerical collars. Once I got a chance to wear one after being ordained, I realized my chaplain supervisor had been right. My voice was not transformed by a costume any more than it was amplified by mimicking my professors.

And as to their so-called sexism, I came to miss the patients' refreshing candor once I was ordained into the polite world of church clergy politics, which mostly had the good manners to keep its sexism to itself.

So much so that later, when I found myself teaching preaching at my alma mater, I was surprised to hear the other students, mostly male, defend the right of a female student to speak so quietly she could barely be heard. "I don't think she should change a thing," they said to my suggestion that her timid, breathy voice was getting in the way of our hearing. "She's just great as she is," they said, as if I had just suggested she look into plastic surgery rather than work on her delivery. And it was then that it first occurred to me that much of the fake sympathy the church gives to women preachers is neither kind nor harmless. Instead it ensures that they will never move out of their small space, never work on that annoying tick, never question the professorial copycat routine that will be meaningless to any listener who wasn't with them in that classroom. In other words, the pretense of admiring a woman's weak preaching voice can sometimes be the very thing that ensures her real voice will never be heard.

And what is that real voice? What do breathing exercises have to do with the breath of God? What role does the vessel play? How do you find your preaching voice without sacrificing your authenticity? When do craft and practice cross the line into entertainment and party tricks? We've all heard the sermon that had more jokes than an after-dinner speaker but no depth. And we've also not heard someone who may well have had something important to say. Was the error in our hearing or in her speaking? Should she change or should we? This book will take you into those questions in concrete and provocative ways. You will hear from a woman who learned to measure her own volume by how loud the men spoke, and to adjust her voice down accordingly. You will hear from a professor who almost didn't write a book on physical voice because of the internal voices that told her no one wanted to hear about it. You will hear about how breath matters as much in preaching as it does in living, and then confront the theological notion that the Holy Spirit works through both.

So when did I find my preaching voice? I found it in the midst of all these hard questions, most valuably explored in the company of my fellow travelers. Just as the call to preach is not individual but requires the body, so does the cultivating of a continuing call. We practice, we do it over and over, hopefully getting better and better, and truer and truer to the Word that gives us life.

If it were as simple as changing costumes, we would all rent that magical authority-bestowing collar, cape, or wand, and no one would have to practice a sermon in front of other people again. If mimicking a mentor worked, the world would be full of straight A students reading from their excellent exams in the voice of a teacher no one else cares about. If it were all about style points, we'd all be reading style manuals.

Instead we just get up and do it again. We practice. We practice preaching. It is both a rehearsal to prepare and our main devotional practice. As a devotional practice, it is never a performance but always an encounter with the divine, who loves us just as we are and knows that we are capable of even more.

And then, in one of those classic Jesus reversals, just when we think we have found our preaching voice, we lose it. Where did it go? Why does this happen?

Sometimes, we get too good at it. It gets too easy. We don't have to reach anymore, and we wonder, what's next? At least the good preachers do, the ones for whom it is always a practice of the faith.

Sometimes our best voice gets lost, due to lack of attention. We've let it go, misplaced it, been too casual with something precious. It takes work to retrieve it from wherever we last left it, perhaps under a pile of administrative tasks no one will ever remember us for.

Most painful are the times when something or someone seems to take your voice away. I believe it happens to every preacher, now that it has happened to me. A personal failure constricts your throat with lumps too large for a quick sip of water. A church system demands your silence, shunning and shaming. Sometimes the inability to speak is self-protective. You are not ready to hear what you have to say. Why would anyone else want to?

And yet the Sunday sermon still rolls around and you have no choice. You speak. Maybe someone else listens. The strong voice you took so long to discover now comes out in squeaks and sighs. At least it sounds that way to you.

We're always learning how to preach again. We always need the practice. So then we do the bravest thing possible. We go out and ask the people how we sound.

"I couldn't hear you," someone will say. And just as we are ready to come up with all the reasons that statement is so unfair, we hear another voice saying something more important.

Listen. Consider it might be true. Isn't what you have to say worth saying? Isn't it worth hearing? Keep practicing. Keep asking what they heard. Because no matter how good the voice, there is not one preacher who has ever been able to pull off this preaching thing alone, all by herself. It's not a solitary, internal practice but one that requires we speak to someone other than ourselves. I think that's why God gave us voices.

LILLIAN DANIEL

Acknowledgments

I have found that my students are always, in some fashion, my teachers. It is a special joy when students become colleagues and then friends. That is the case with many women who have been my students, whose courage and faith have inspired me in my ministry. It is my prayer that this book will honor them: my students, my teachers, my colleagues, my friends.

I am grateful to the William B. Eerdmans Publishing Company for its continuing confidence in me, and to acquisitions editor Michael Thomson for encouraging me to submit the proposal for this book and for his guidance toward submission. Jennifer Hoffman, the senior project editor, and Lisa Eary, the copyeditor, contributed significantly to the quality and clarity of the book. The speed with which they moved the project through production was impressive.

Sharon Omens graciously granted permission for her painting of Miriam leading the women in song and dance, originally conceived as a painted silk tallit, to be used on the cover of the book. The discovery of her painting with its vibrant colors, the lack of concrete facial detail, and the embodied joy of the women concluded a months-long search for an image that brought to life how I imagined Miriam. Sharon's Miriam could be any woman who joyfully embodies her witness to the goodness of God. For more of Sharon's work, see http://www.sharonomens.com/tallit-beshalach/talit_miriam/.

Palmer Theological Seminary in Philadelphia, Pennsylvania, was the home of my first faculty position. I left Palmer in 2001 after ten years of teaching, but the women I met there never left me. They are at the heart and soul of this book.

Princeton Theological Seminary has provided immeasurable support in teaching environment and opportunities, sabbatical leave, encouragement from administration and colleagues, and fantastic students. President Craig Barnes has been enormously supportive of the faculty and an encouragement to me. The Engle Institute of Preaching has provided the opportunity to work with many experienced women preachers who are eager both to identify their issues with voice and to work on the development of their authentic voices. I am grateful for my colleagues in the Preaching, Worship, and Speech Communication in Ministry area of the Practical Theology Department who are wonderful conversation partners and treasured partners in our mutual teaching ministry: Cleophus LaRue, Sally Brown, James Kay, and especially my colleagues in speech, Michael Brothers and Charles Bartow. In an increasingly technological world, I believe our work in speech communication in ministry that focuses on the authentic human voice is more important than ever, and I am honored to be a part of carrying it forward.

My teaching assistant for the last three years leading to the writing of this book, Samantha Gilmore, has been one of those student-colleague-teacher-friend persons to whom I am indebted. Her dedication and advanced study at the Linklater Center for Voice and Language have improved my own teaching.

There are more women to thank than I can name, and to name any is to miss many. From California and Washington to Philadelphia, PA, and Plainsboro and Princeton, NJ, they have challenged me, loved me, prayed for me, counseled me, walked with me, encouraged me, and put up with me. All have demonstrated a strength of personality that has inspired me over the long journey of bringing this book to fruition. And, of course, my profound gratitude goes to Chatty Cathy, Sarah, Christine, Gi, and Atara, all of whom the reader will meet in the following pages.

In the final stages of writing, I engaged Heather Faller, a former speech student, graduate of Princeton Seminary, and immensely talented writer and editor, to provide substantive editing for the completion of the book. With her superb skills, knowledge of my teaching, and uncanny intuition about my own voice and the intentions of my heart, Heather nudged me ever so wisely toward the best possible expression of my thinking. Thank you, Heather.

This book is dedicated to my two extraordinarily wonderful daughters, Anna and Abby. During the long incubation of this book, they grew up. They have loved me, taught me, and cheered me on. Anna and Abby are now pursuing their own lives and careers, each with a strong, authentic, truth-speaking voice of her own. I could not love them more or be more proud of them. Girls, this is for you.

NANCY LAMMERS GROSS
Princeton, New Jersey

Introduction

The seeds of this book were planted fully fourteen years ago when the reach of my concern for women's voices in preaching far exceeded my understanding of the issue. The basic outline of the book was proposed to a publisher whose editor was enthusiastic about the book, but with one small caveat that required a "tweak," she said. Her only reservation was that my voice was not in my book proposal on women and voice. My voice, Nancy's voice, was not in my book proposal on women's voices in preaching. The editor thought I could address this concern with a "tweak." But for me it was an existential crisis. How could it be that someone who hardly knew me could detect that my authentic voice was not in my writing? I became sufficiently paralyzed by this observation and what it meant in my own life that I had to put the book on a back burner. I went on to serve six years as dean of student life at Princeton Seminary, and only four years ago did I begin to think about returning to the project.

When I addressed the project full time during a sabbatical leave, I realized that the issue of my voice was critical to my ability to write this book. And I realized that I had found my voice. Every time I got stuck in the writing, I came to discover that I had stopped using my natural conversational teaching and speech workshop voice and was reluctant to say what I knew. When I resumed writing in the voice I use in my everyday work and claimed my own convictions, the material flowed. I believe you will hear my voice in this book. The freedom I experienced when I found my voice is God's gift to every Christian, male and female. I hope you will hear my voice and be inspired to pursue the freedom to speak, whatever the effort and education required. God has called you to speak, and the church needs your voice to be heard.

Women were ordained to preach in my denomination, the Presbyterian Church (USA) in 1956. But when I was growing up, I never heard an ordained woman preach. I had only seen one woman in the pulpit by the time I got to seminary. No one ever told me I could be a minister of the gospel, or even more specifically a preacher—but no one ever told me I couldn't. When I made my call and intentions known to my pastors, I received full support. My call to preach overpowered the lack of evidence for women's right to preach, and I simply followed that call. But over the years, I came to realize that not everyone experienced the support that I had. Many women before me and with me, many women after me, and many women still today have had to fight difficult battles to win a way into the pulpit to which God called them.

My generation began to populate the churches with ordained women, and even preaching women—in small churches, of course. When I began to teach preaching, worship, and speech in the early 1990s, I thought that young women would come to seminary more empowered and emboldened to preach and lead in worship than women of my generation had when I attended seminary in the late 1970s, simply because so many of these women had known women as pastors. It confused me greatly to see that young women were, by and large, even less emboldened, less empowered, than women of my generation. I asked myself, *What is going on here?*

The answers are as numerous as the women seeking to follow their call into the church, and the issues reside with women of all ages and circumstances, of all racial and ethnic backgrounds. There were no one or two stories that explained everyone's circumstances, but there were common themes. I began asking and listening and mentally tracking these stories. I came to learn that nearly every woman had a story related to her voice, and that it was important that I listen not only to her physical voice, but also to the story that voice was telling. It dawned on me that a woman's struggle to use her voice went well beyond permission-giving in a particular ecclesial context. I realized that her struggle went well beyond the measure of her conviction. Listening to women's stories was one of the most important dimensions of my teaching ministry.

This book is the result of my work with women over the course of a twenty-five year teaching ministry, of listening to the stories of women who have struggled to employ their voices in the proclamation of the Word. It addresses the tendency for women—even women of strong call, conviction, and gifts—to apologize with their bodies and their physical voices for presuming to preach or lead in worship, or for simply occupying pulpit or chancel space.

Many women struggle to speak, to use their physical voices, for various reasons. For some there is simply a disconnect between the woman's self-understanding as a preacher and her own body. She cannot connect the shape and size or the femaleness of her body with her image of what a preacher is or what a preacher looks like. Some have not yet discovered their public voice; a woman in this situation does not realize she has a dimension of her voice that is suitable for speaking in a public context, or she knows she has that voice but thinks it is inappropriate to use it. Some have had their voices silenced by forces outside of their control; someone or something in their past has told them not to use their voice. Some cannot love their own bodies, or even accept their own bodies, and since the voice is a full-body instrument, they have no access to their actual speaking voices. Some women's bodies have come under such verbal and physical assault that they can only assume a physical posture of defense, a posture from which they cannot speak with any confidence.

I know women who can sing powerfully, but when it is time to speak, especially to speak the Word of God, their voices can barely make it to the microphone.

I know women who, when they are in the company of other women, have voices that are full: full of laughter, full of body, full of personality. But when they are in the company of men, their voices are small, subdued, without mirth, and seem to fade into the background to avoid attracting attention.

I know women who can write brilliantly, poetically, compellingly, articulately, powerfully. But when it comes to speaking, rendering, and preaching what they have written, their voices are without imagination or range or power or authority.

I know women who have fire for the gospel pent up in their bones, but since they are not allowed to preach from the pulpits of their own churches, they have shrunk their voices to fit the size of their assigned roles.

I know women who have been told that they are so very *nice*, but their voices are so (fill in the blank): unpleasant, high, soft, tiny, screechy, muddled . . .

I know women who have insightful and important things to say, but who cannot say them with the conviction they feel.

This book is for these women, and for the people who love them and who teach them, and for men who also struggle with these issues. This book will address the question of why many women struggle to speak up. Of why is it so difficult for many women to claim their space in the pulpit and to venture to speak with the strength of conviction that matches their call and the content of their hearts. And of how women can learn to use their physical voices in preaching.

For the purposes of this book, I am denoting the literal, physical speaking voice as "voice" with a lower case "v." The word "voice" may frequently appear in the plural form—women's voices.

The term "Voice," with an upper case "V," will refer to the metaphorical Voice; that is, a woman's perspective as expressed in a sermon, for example. "Voice" with an upper case "V" and in the singular will refer more broadly to the entitlement to speak, to the right to articulate one's viewpoint, one's perspective on a biblical text or experience in the world. The term "Voice" will not refer to the actual physical speaking voice; it is not the sound that emits from a woman's body.

This book is primarily *not* about Voice. It is primarily not about women's perspectives or experiences in the world that give rise to interpretations of text and life that may vary from men's. This book is primarily not an apologetic for women's right to speak and to preach and to lead in the public worship of God. Though in practice these matters are important and not yet settled, they are covered elsewhere and are assumed in my work. That is, women's right to preach is not up for debate here; it is claimed.[1]

This book is about the voice, the woman's voice, women's voices, the instrument we use to physically and verbally, orally, *out loud* proclaim the Word of God in public worship, in the public sphere, and in more private dimensions of ministry. This book explores the question, *Why can't more women just speak up?*

The governing thesis of this book is the following:

The voice is a full-body instrument.
Many women struggle to speak.
Many women struggle to speak because they are disconnected from their bodies.

Women have trouble speaking because they are disconnected from their bodies. The voice is a full-body, physical, and musical instrument. When I use the terms "full-body instrument" or "full-body voice" or "embodied voice," I am referring to the need for the entire physical body to be employed in the production of vocal sound. The physical voice is not just a larynx and a mouth; the motor for the voice is not the chest and lungs alone. Properly used, the voice is a foot-to-head instrument, a full-body instrument. It is precisely women's bodies, however, that make women doubt themselves and feel apologetic or too self-conscious to be effective in the public performance of the Word. When women are disconnected from their bodies, they are disconnected from their voices. No matter how profound the Voice, the perspective, if a woman cannot use her voice, if she cannot be heard or understood, the impact of the Voice will be diminished, and even, at times, moot.

Many women are disconnected from their bodies, and therefore from their voices. The result in the pulpit is often tiny, apologetic, breathy, little-girl voices, or ever-present smiles, or nervous, compromising, inappropriate laughter, or the all-pervasive upward inflection at the end of sentences. I call this small-sounding voice the *disembodied voice*. The voice that is produced by the full body, the connected voice, is the *embodied voice*.

The underlying theological claim assumed in this work has to do with the incarnation and the doctrine of creation. God created humanity male and female. God's Word dwells in us, male and female. God declares the woman's body good and calls women to make full use of their full-body instruments in the proclamation of the gospel. This call to use her body is issued without asking how much a woman weighs, or what size clothing she wears, or whether she measures up to cultural expectations of the good woman's body or the woman's good body. This call to use one's body is valid even if that body has been abused.

Here I must pause to say that not everything that can be said about women can be said of all women, and not of some men, just as not everything that can be said about men can be said of all men, and not of some women. I focus on women in this book because I have found that women have specific and peculiar challenges in using their voices, and working with women to free their voices is a calling in and of itself. I also want to address those readers who do not use the audible speaking voice and to whom sound may not be accessible. One of the students who best manifested my understanding of the embodied voice was a member of the deaf community. This man and I used to talk about how I wanted my hearing students to be as bodily invested in their communication as he was. He demonstrated to me the power of the truly embodied voice, even when there is no audible sound.[2]

The biblical mandate or metaphor that grounds this work is the story of Miriam, what I call "The Symphony of Miriam." Miriam's voice, that is her literal speaking voice, is instrumental to the story of salvation. Some would argue that even though ancient biblical editors and redactors may have sought to minimize or even eliminate Miriam's voice, she could not be silenced. It could be the case that the opposite is true, that the fight was to preserve Miriam's story because she was so crucial to the nation of Israel and the story of salvation.

Chapter 1 is "The Symphony of Miriam." Four biblical texts feature Miriam, Miriam's voice, and her participation in the story of salvation. God used Miriam to deliver the people of Israel from Egypt, from the house of bondage, and to lead them to the Promised Land.

We will discuss what these stories tell us about God's call to women, how women are instrumental in the work of God, and how women's full bodies are the instruments that are played.

Chapter 2, "Asking Permission," tells the stories of women I have worked with over the years. These stories are paradigmatic; they are unique as personal and individual stories, but they easily represent dimensions of many women's stories. Three of the stories are told by the women themselves, in their own words, under the pseudonym of each one's choosing. The stories testify to the kinds of life experiences that lead women to lose connection to their bodies and to their voices.

I will address challenges faced more specifically by many Korean and African American women as well. Women from these communities often have additional issues that arise out of their particular racial, ethnic, and ecclesial traditions. These issues are a consequence of their specific cultural milieu, which often puts women in a position of subservience to men, and/or from the fact that their faith communities often add a biblical or theological prohibition against women using their voices to proclaim the Word of God. Again, there is no pretense that these stories speak for all Korean women, or all African American women. But they feature dynamics common to many of the women I have worked with.

Chapter 3 is "Voice Lost." We will look at three predominant reasons why women are disconnected from their bodies in order to determine how and why women have so much trouble claiming their physical voices and their space in public speaking. The first reason is that many women are engaged in a constant wrestling match with their own bodies. Women try to *whip* their bodies into shape, *fight* their weight, and *struggle* to understand the connection of their bodies to their selves. Women do not receive the message that they should love their body no matter the shape and size. The loudest messages telling them to love their bodies come from weight loss clinics, products, and promotions, which tell them their bodies are not okay. Nowhere is the message to love their bodies proclaimed louder than the message most women have received—that their bodies are unacceptable.

The second reason we will consider for why women are disconnected from their bodies is the silencing of their Voice, the loss of their right to speak their perspective, what they understand to be the truth of their own experience. When a woman has been deprived of her right to speak what she understands as the truth of her own experience, it often becomes difficult for her to speak at all.

The third reason we will consider for why women are disconnected from their bodies has to do with experiences of physical or sexual abuse. We will examine the ways in which abuse can lead a woman to disconnect from her body and the kinds of obstacles this disconnection creates to using her voice to speak.

The purpose of this chapter is to draw the connection between the messages women receive from an early age about their bodies, the silencing of women's perspectives and the lack of permission they experience, and the risk of abuse associated with being female, and women's inability to employ their voices as full-body instruments in the service of the proclamation of the gospel. This consideration of the besieged body that leads to the voice lost will prepare us for thinking about how we can again access our bodies in order to exercise our full-body instruments.

Chapter 4, "Voice Restored," will look at the importance of knowing and accepting who you are as foundational to using your voice. Chapter 2 presents the stories of several women whose actual vocal production was compromised by receiving the message that they did not have permission to speak. In chapter 4, we will look at the need to focus on the call of God to ministry as all the permission-giving anyone needs to exercise their voice in service to the reconciling ministry of Jesus Christ in the church and in the world. I will tell my own story about how I struggled to come to grips with this self-knowledge; then I will begin to build back for all of us the confidence and permission to speak. In claiming this female voice as good, we will discuss what it means to "body forth" as a theological imperative of preaching the gospel, and what bodying forth requires of preachers.

Finally, we will look briefly at the physiology of the female voice and how it actually differs from that of the male voice. Researchers ask the question, *Is there a female vocal cord?* The differences are not dramatic, but they are worth noting since they coincide with women's physical and psychological development, especially at adolescence and menopause. The particularities of the female voice also highlight significant self-care needs and issues.

Chapter 5, "Embodied Voice," is the constructive resolution. A self-reflection exercise will lead the reader through the story of her own voice and is followed by exercises for discovering and developing the full-body voice. We will also discuss what a full-body voice sounds like.

Chapter 6, "As If It Matters," is a reader's workshop on John 11:1–44, followed by a sermon based on the oral rendering of the story of the raising of Lazarus. Martha and Mary, two women who were close friends of Jesus, freely use their voices to express to him their disappointment, anger, grief, and hope. Their emotional honesty and willingness to express their own internal truth, the truth of their own experience is a model of authentic, embodied communication. An embodied understanding of the women's voices leads to an embodied gospel sermon.

Writing a book on voice is a difficult matter, because sound matters. If the reader would like to see and hear the exercises in chapters 5 and 6, and hear the sermon in chapter 6, please visit www.Nancy LammersGross.com.

CHAPTER 1

The Symphony of Miriam

There are many women in the Bible who can provide us with a model for the ways, the times, and the circumstances in which they used their voices. Ruth spoke immortal lines of commitment:

> Where you go, I will go;
>   where you lodge, I will lodge;
> your people shall be my people;
>   and your God my God. (Ruth 1:16b)

Esther courageously hatched a plan for the salvation of her people, putting her own life on the line with the offense of going before the king without invitation:

> Go, gather all the Jews to be found in Susa, and hold a fast on
> my behalf, and neither eat nor drink for three days, night or day.
> I and my maids will also fast as you do. After that I will go to
> the king, though it is against the law; and if I perish, I perish.
> (Esther 4:16)

Deborah, a judge in Israel, developed a battle plan, gave orders, and commanded troops. When she laid out the battle plan to her senior officer, Barak, he said, "If you go with me, I will go; but if you will not go with me, I will not go" (Judg. 4:8). The men did not want to go into battle without her. Such was the power and esteem of Deborah. I am curious about her tone of voice when she replied,

I

I will surely go with you; nevertheless, the road on which you are going will not lead to your glory, for the Lord will sell Sisera into the hand of a woman. (Judg. 4:9)

In John, it was Mary Magdalene, of course, who first gave witness to the resurrection:

I have seen the Lord. (John 20:18)

There are many women in the Bible, but I have chosen Miriam as our biblical witness because the arc of her life is told in the stories of Scripture. She must have been just a girl when she watched over her baby brother, Moses, in the bulrushes. And her story ends at her death after wandering for a generation in the wilderness with the Israelites. The four episodes in which Miriam is a prominent witness to the work of God are substantive; they literally have body. All four episodes involve Miriam's body. Not only is Miriam's voice heard; her body is fully engaged. As I studied these texts, I was not interested in developing a second-level reflection on the way women's voices are used in the Bible. Rather, I wanted to catch a biblical woman in the act of using her voice and to discover the impact that had on those around her. It was a confirming surprise to discover that it is not only Miriam's voice, her words, head, and heart that are involved in her stories, but her physical body as well. Miriam became a witness to how women live in their bodies, the risks they take, and the full-bodied witness they make. Miriam gave her body to her ministry, and when things went wrong, she took the consequences in her body.

When I began to work with the Miriam texts, I was enthralled with the idea of speaking for Miriam. I hoped to capture her voice, the depth of her faith, the richness of her experience, to speak from her, not just about her. In homiletical jargon, if this chapter was a sermon, we might call the form "first-person narrative." Of course, we cannot capture Miriam's actual oral speech. We cannot know the pitch or tenor of her voice, though we can guess at the tone by what she says. We know that she was intelligent, bold, spontaneous, righteous, and absolutely crucial to the life of the wandering Israelites. But after all my work with the Miriam texts, I found that I still do not know Miriam well enough to speak for her. It is not that so little is said about Miriam in Scripture; it is that so little says so much, and there is much more again still to be heard. This is humbling.

Therefore, we will not hear Miriam's voice in the first person in this chapter, but we will hear the symphony of her testimony, a symphony as rich and sonorous as any found in Scripture. And when we get to the end of the final movement, I believe we will not want her symphony to end, but will want it to be drawn out in long, resounding, bold strokes of victorious testimony and praise.

The *Symphony* of Miriam is meant to contrast what is traditionally called the *Song* of Miriam. The Scripture tells us that Miriam led the women in song and dance with tambourines after crossing the Red Sea, celebrating and worshiping God for deliverance from the Egyptians. Scripture attributes to Miriam a one-line, unison song of joy and triumph. This is the song of Miriam:

Sing to the LORD, for he has triumphed gloriously;
horse and rider he has thrown into the sea. (Exod. 15:21)

There are four texts in which Miriam is featured. Her story can be heard as a symphony with four movements.

> Movement I: Exodus 2:1-10—Miriam watches out for her baby brother
> Movement II: Exodus 15:19-21—Miriam leads celebration after crossing the Red Sea
> Movement III: Numbers 12:1-16—Miriam and Aaron object to Moses's marriage
> Movement IV: Numbers 20:1-2—Miriam dies, and there is no water in that place

Traditionally, a symphony is a musical composition requiring a full orchestra with woodwind, string, brass, and percussion instruments. Especially since the eighteenth century, the symphony has typically been defined by four movements: an opening movement that sounds the major themes of the piece and is fast tempo, a second movement that is slower and more stately, a third movement that is dance-like at medium/fast tempo, and a fourth movement that is faster again and has a pattern of repeating themes.

While Miriam's symphony does not correlate directly to the traditional symphonic form, the stories in the four primary texts in which Miriam is featured form her own unique symphony.

For its recurring theme of water, Miriam's symphony might be called Water Music.

For tradition's memory of the first movement as a story only about baby Moses, Miriam's symphony reminds us of Tchaikovsky's Fourth Symphony, with the lone French horn sounding the opening theme, but with fantastic complexities to come.

For the importance of voices in the stories, it could be like Beethoven's Ninth Symphony, the first written with the use of a chorus of voices.

But this is Miriam's symphony. The first movement is brief, but contains all the major themes of the symphony:

– the terroristic tactics of the Pharaoh in proclaiming that all Jewish baby boys should be murdered;
– the theme of water as baby Moses is placed in the river;
– the complex relationship of sister to brother, Miriam to Moses;
– how Moses's loyalty to his people is forged;
– the dimension of difficult ethnic relationships: Moses to his Egyptian mother and Moses to a Cushite woman;
– the theme of salvation.

The second movement in Miriam's symphony actually has a quicker tempo. The people Israel are given release from the house of bondage, but joy turns to panic when the Pharaoh changes his mind and sends his soldiers after the people. The waters that could pose the ultimate danger become a vehicle for salvation; there is dancing and joy and the rehearsal of a new story of salvation.

The third movement is dance-like. But it is not a happy dance,

4

and it is not a "joke" as the symphonic form scherzo might suggest.[1] Miriam and Aaron dance around the issues with their brother Moses, at times being more and less direct. One can imagine the four figures in the dance: Miriam, Aaron, Moses, and God, each stepping out to perform a solo, as the complexity of themes and unknown resolution build in tension.

The fourth movement gives the resolution for which we long, but it is not the outcome we want or expect. The themes of water, relationship, salvation, and leadership all overlap like waves on a beach, and in the end, we learn that God's way will prevail with the people, but not in the way we would have planned.[2]

Exodus 2:1–10

Now a man from the house of Levi went and married a Levite woman. [2]The woman conceived and bore a son; and when she saw that he was a fine baby, she hid him three months. [3]When she could hide him no longer she got a papyrus basket for him, and plastered it with bitumen and pitch; she put the child in it and placed it among the reeds on the bank of the river. [4]His sister stood at a distance, to see what would happen to him.

[5]The daughter of Pharaoh came down to bathe at the river, while her attendants walked beside the river. She saw the basket among the reeds and sent her maid to bring it. [6]When she opened it, she saw the child. He was crying, and she took pity on him. "This must be one of the Hebrews' children," she said. [7]Then his sister said to Pharaoh's daughter, "Shall I go and get you a nurse from the Hebrew women to nurse the child for you?" [8]Pharaoh's daughter said to her, "Yes." So the girl went and called the child's mother. [9]Pharaoh's daughter said to her, "Take this child and nurse it for me, and I will give you your wages." So the woman took the child and nursed it. [10]When the child grew up, she brought him to Pharaoh's daughter, and she took him as her son. She named him Moses, "because," she said, "I drew him out of the water."

The first movement of the symphony is one of the most familiar stories in Scripture. Traditionally, it is considered a story about baby Moses. In one of the storybooks we read to our children, baby Moses's sister does not even make an appearance, and the baby's mother has a very limited role. There is one lone primary star of the story: Moses. This is odd, since the baby Moses has no functionality in the story, no agency, no *instrumentality*. He is entirely passive. When we simplify a story, we leave out the characters we deem unimportant; in this case all of those lesser characters are female.

I have never heard Exodus 2:1-10 referred to as "A Story about the Love of a Sister." Nor have I heard it referred to as "Pharaoh's Daughter Saves a Baby," or "Mother Becomes Nursemaid to Her Own Child for Wages." Far more interesting still would be "Two Women, Two Ethnicities Collude to Save a Baby Boy," or "Pharaoh's Brutal Plan to Wipe Out Jews Paves Path to Own Destruction." Well, those are too long for the name of a story, but the point is clear. Women play the key roles, but it is a story about the passive baby boy.

The story of Miriam is the story of many in our midst. It is the story of one whose life and work is always overshadowed by some allegedly more important figure, often a man.

Miriam's is the sonata of one whose creativity and power of personality were not recognized or valued as highly as the gifts of others.

The Symphony of Miriam carries the haunting strains of one whose God-given gifts may have been first opened and first broken, but were never used as much as the favored gifts given to the men in her life.

The first movement opens with our heroine in an anonymous role that is entirely overshadowed by the destiny of the baby boy in the bulrushes. So long has baby Moses been the centerpiece of the story that we lose sight of the fact that it is the women in the story who defy the earthly power of the Pharaoh, who listen instead to the power of love and the power of the mother-child bond within their hearts. The power of love in these women's lives is the gift of God. The power of this love is the gift of God that enabled the Exodus. The power of God is exercised through these women, who show themselves, in this circumstance, to be a greater threat to the Pharaoh's designs than the men.

6

A sister stands at a distance to see what will become of her baby brother. I can't help but think of all the sisters who watch over their brothers and sisters to see that they get up in the morning, all the sisters who watch over their brothers and sisters to see that they get to school and get home from school, who see that they get dinner and stay out of trouble. There is a sister on every street today, in every neighborhood, in every church who is carrying out this ministry of love.

A big sister watches over her baby brother to see what will become of him, and when the one who has the power to shape his future enters the scene, the unnamed sister steps forward on her own initiative to offer a plan. There is nothing in the story to suggest that Miriam had this plan in mind when she went to the river's edge to see what would happen to her baby brother, nor do we find any hint that her mother hoped one day to nurse her own baby Moses again. We are only told that Miriam stood at a distance to see what would become of her brother. We do not know how old Miriam was, but I try to imagine how this girl, a slave, had the courage to walk up to a princess, the Pharaoh's daughter. Approaching the Pharaoh's daughter required not just love for her brother, but some level of moral and physical courage; it could even have posed bodily risk to Miriam.

Miriam physically approached power. I am sure it was not unusual for a Hebrew girl to be lingering at water's edge; it would have been the girls' and the women's job to gather water and to wash the clothes. Miriam probably drew no attention to herself as she stood at a distance. So deeply imbedded in our collective consciousness is the outcome of this story that probably few imagine other possible scenarios. An Egyptian soldier could have come upon the baby and drowned him in obedience to the Pharaoh's orders. A lesser Egyptian woman could have found him and taken him away to be raised in anonymity, lost forever to Miriam and her family. Miriam did not know the outcome, and she surely did not imagine herself coming face to face with Pharaoh's daughter.

Miriam physically approached power, and then she spoke to power. The plan was brilliant, spontaneous, simple, even logical, and probably not all that unusual. Slave playing nursemaid to power's progeny is an age-old practice. Miriam's plan, however, also included a bit of subterfuge, as only she knew her plan would unite baby with mother.

Miriam did not know the outcome of the story; we can only imagine other outcomes of the story. God, however, had a plan, and the plan involved the bodily presence of a slave girl. The plan of this still-anonymous sister would forever bond the baby to his native people, and yet would also give him the position of privilege from which he would one day rise up.

"Why don't I get you a Hebrew woman to nurse the child?" "Yes, why don't you? And when he is weaned, I will take him for my son and raise him up." In her book *Just a Sister Away*, Renita Weems examines the relationships of women in the Bible who share a story, such as the relationships between Miriam and her Cushite sister-in-law, between Hagar and Sarah, between Naomi and Ruth, and between Elizabeth and Mary.[3] We will hear more about Miriam's relationship to Moses's wife in the discussion of Numbers 12:1-16, but I have to wonder how this first movement in Miriam's symphony unfolded. What kind of relationship did Miriam have with Pharaoh's daughter? Did Moses's mother meet Pharaoh's daughter? Did Miriam give regular reports to Pharaoh's daughter and perhaps even take the baby to visit her? Did Miriam continue to collude in hiding the fact that a Hebrew baby boy would become the Pharaoh's grandson? It was years before this story actually became about Moses, and during all that time, the untold story was about the women and their commitment to love the child. Phyllis Trible observes that "If Pharaoh had recognized the power of women, he might well have reversed his decree and had daughters killed rather than sons. But God moves in mysterious ways."[4] This is an apt observation for each movement in *The Symphony of Miriam*.

God's plan of salvation runs like an arrow straight through this big sister, through her body and her voice. She stands at the water's edge, and by her actions she is both an instrument in God's saving design and a testimony to God's love. At the end of this first movement in *The Symphony of Miriam*, the Scripture has not yet even told us her name.

The Symphony of Miriam

Exodus 15:19–21

When the horses of Pharaoh with his chariots and his chariot drivers went into the sea, the LORD brought back the waters of the sea upon them; but the Israelites walked through the sea on dry ground. ²⁰Then the prophet Miriam, Aaron's sister, took a tambourine in her hand; and all the women went out after her with tambourines and with dancing. ²¹And Miriam sang to them:

> "Sing to the LORD, for he has triumphed gloriously;
> horse and rider he has thrown into the sea."

The second movement of Miriam's symphony, unlike that of most symphonies, is the most familiar movement, at least insofar as it concerns Miriam. We do not hear from Moses's sister or about her while Moses grows and the Hebrew people groan under the weight of their bondage. But we know by the theme of the second movement that Miriam too has grown in stature and in power and influence with her people.

Miriam's song holds an awkward place in Exodus 15, coming just after the Song of the Sea, a beautiful and lengthy song of victorious praise supposedly rendered by a stuttering and inarticulate Moses along with "the Israelites." One can just imagine this exhausted and traumatized people, narrowly escaping Pharaoh's chariots with their lives, bursting into an eloquent song that recounts the whole experience. It has become widely held by scholars that Miriam's song in Exodus 15:19–21 is the older, more original fragment.

Coming at the end of the Song of the Sea, Miriam's song suddenly recapitulates God's saving act at the Red Sea and is a spontaneous expression of joyous thanksgiving. It is difficult to imagine a scene in which Moses would give his long speech, and then Miriam would spontaneously jump into action with song and dance. It is far easier to imagine the spontaneous celebration as the people watch the Pharaoh's horses and riders thrown into the sea, and the people discover themselves safe on the other side.

While Moses's Song of the Sea is ascribed to a later editor who wanted Moses to be the first to interpret theologically what God had done and to thank God for it, its eloquence begs the question of its authenticity.[5] When we are praying and singing and praising God freely and spontaneously in the Spirit, we don't always sound like polished, tall-steeple church preachers. We certainly don't expect this kind of polished speech from Moses, who argued with God that he could not do the speaking God wanted him to do. In fact, Aaron was appointed, in part, to speak in Moses's stead.

Miriam, now recognized in the Scriptures as a prophet herself, leads the women in praise and thanksgiving, and shows the rest of the congregation how to worship God. With her dancing, Miriam embodies praise and worship. Miriam leads the women in dance and in song, the Scripture tells us, but her act is so bold that I wonder if there were not others who followed her lead . . . the children, perhaps the men.[6] Otherwise, why would a song also be attributed to Moses?

Miriam embodies courage when she approaches the Pharaoh's daughter about baby Moses. Miriam embodies the love of God in praise and thanksgiving as she leads the women in song and dance.

The waters of the sea could have been the instrument of death for the Israelites, just as the waters of the river could have been the instrument of death for baby Moses. Both became waters of salvation, by themselves neither a blessing nor a curse, and both are an opportunity for Miriam to testify to God's saving intervention in the lives of his people. The second movement of *The Symphony of Miriam* closes with the strains of a beautiful melody, haunting in its simplicity and resounding with the spontaneity of sheer joy.[7]

Numbers 12:1–16

While they were at Hazeroth, Miriam and Aaron spoke against Moses because of the Cushite woman whom he had married (for he had indeed married a Cushite woman); [2]and they said, "Has the LORD spoken only through Moses? Has he not spoken through us also?" And the LORD heard it. [3]Now the man Moses was very humble, more so than anyone else on the face of the earth. Suddenly the LORD said to Moses, Aaron, and Miriam, "Come out, you three, to the tent of meeting." So the three of them came out. Then the LORD came down in a pillar of cloud, and stood at the entrance of the tent, and called Aaron and Miriam; and they both came forward. And he said, "Hear my words:

> When there are prophets among you,
>> I the LORD make myself known to them in visions;
>> I speak to them in dreams.
> Not so with my servant Moses;
>> he is entrusted with all my house.
> With him I speak face to face—clearly, not in riddles;
>> and he beholds the form of the LORD.

Why then were you not afraid to speak against my servant Moses?" And the anger of the LORD was kindled against them, and he departed.

[10]When the cloud went away from over the tent, Miriam had become leprous, as white as snow. And Aaron turned towards Miriam and saw that she was leprous. [11]Then Aaron said to Moses, "Oh, my lord, do not punish us for a sin that we have so foolishly committed. [12]Do not let her be like one stillborn, whose flesh is half consumed when it comes out of its mother's womb." [13]And Moses cried to the LORD, "O God, please heal her." [14]But the LORD said to Moses, "If her father had but spit in her face, would she not bear her shame for seven days? Let her be shut out of the camp for seven days, and after that she may be brought in again." [15]So Miriam was shut out of the camp for seven days; and the people did not set out on the march until Miriam had been brought in again. [16]After that the people set out from Hazeroth, and camped in the wilderness of Paran.

The third movement of Miriam's symphony in Numbers 12 develops like so many third movements. The themes are various; they are intertwined; the hearer cannot always tell which section of the orchestra has which theme. There is sibling rivalry, jealousy toward a new sister-in-law, perhaps racial tension, punishment and repentance, healing and restoration.

Miriam and Aaron go to their brother Moses and ask for a meeting. It seems that Miriam is the one who criticizes Moses about the nature of his mixed marriage. Moses had married a "Cushite" woman. The precise nature of this offense isn't exactly clear, but the possibilities seem to range from "he married someone of a different color" to "he married outside the 'church.'" The cultural and pastoral issues of inclusivity, exclusivity, and diversity are as old as Scripture itself.

Renita Weems reflects fruitfully on the possible tensions involved in the relationship of sister to sister-in-law. Miriam's star clearly rose from her early anonymity at river's edge to recognition as a prophet and worship leader at the edge of the sea, to becoming, perhaps, Moses's right-hand woman. In a culture where it was difficult for a woman to achieve social status on her own, Miriam would have held special status as Moses's sister. Weems imagines the access Miriam would have had to Moses before he was married to this woman, and how Miriam's special counsel may not have been as needed as it had been before. Miriam seemed to lead the way in righteous indignation at Moses's choice of a spouse.

We aren't sure whether Miriam or Aaron led the way on the second recrimination, but if it wasn't bad enough, in their minds, that Moses had married this unacceptable person, they can't resist asking, "Has the LORD spoken only through Moses? Has he not spoken through us also?"

I can hear the wheels turning: "We're preachers too. Why does the favored brother get all the attention, all the devotion from the people, all the credit?"

Is this sibling rivalry? Sour grapes? Insubordination? Or is it an honest, justifiable protest from a brother and sister to whom God had also spoken, and through whom God had also chosen to work?

Whatever the motive behind the accusations of Miriam and Aaron, Moses was a humble man, and he did not defend himself. Moses didn't have to. He had God for a personal protection plan. And God called out Miriam and Aaron, out of the camp of the congregation to the tent of meeting. And God came to them in a pillar of cloud and demonstrated to them beyond a shadow of a doubt God's sovereignty.

Tradition has it that Miriam must somehow have committed the greater offense because she received the greater punishment. Aaron got a tongue-lashing; Miriam got leprosy. But I have to wonder if it is as simple as that.

If this story is true, an accurate account of an actual event in the life of the wandering nation of Israel, then perhaps it is the case that Miriam's offense was no greater than Aaron's, but rather that God expected more of her. Perhaps the one who had been so instrumental in enabling the life of Moses, and who was so cued in to the activity of God that she was the first to sing God's praise after crossing the Red Sea, perhaps this one should have known better than to stand in the way of God's plan. And for that, God punished her.

But some say this story is a fabrication that takes into account Miriam's legendary leprosy, the fact that there was some sibling rivalry among the three, and that Moses did, in fact, marry someone not of the nation Israel. If this is the case, if the story is merely a fabrication, then perhaps Miriam receives the greater punishment at the hand of this storyteller because Miriam is the greater threat. Perhaps Miriam challenging Moses was perceived to be a greater threat than Aaron challenging Moses.[8]

In any event, Miriam clearly seems to get the raw end of the deal. Yet once again, Miriam is used by God to testify to God's absolute resolve that nothing and no one will stand in the way of God's determined plan of salvation for God's people. Like the unmistakable sound of a trumpet piercing through the themes and variations played out in other sections, Miriam is instrumental in God's plan. And if she will not fully cooperate, she will be used instrumentally as a sign to all others for generations to come: do not interfere with the plan of the Lord.

Deuteronomy 24:8–9 tells us to be careful to follow the law and "Remember what the LORD your God did to Miriam on your journey out of Egypt." Miriam isn't just instrumental; she becomes paradigmatic.

Miriam physically approached power at the edge of the river; she physically praised God in song and dance at the edge of the Red Sea. And here, she takes the punishment of God in the flesh. She takes it in her body. Aaron got yelled at; Miriam got leprosy, a death sentence of a disease. Not only did she take the punishment bodily, but she was then bodily isolated from the larger body, the community, the nation, her people. Leprosy spells separation. The female leader, who was so crucial to the heart of her people's mission, meanderings, and future ministry, was physically, bodily quarantined from the people. This isolation amounts to a death sentence just as much as the disease itself.

At Moses's pleading, God commutes Miriam's sentence from death by disease and isolation to only seven days of isolation, after which she could return to the people following purification rites.

In the third movement the water theme is barely discernable. We know, however, as the third movement concludes, that Miriam would have had to engage in a ritual of water cleansing before being pronounced purified and able to come back into the congregation, the congregation that waited for her return. Only when Miriam was healed of her leprosy, purified, and returned to her community did the nation continue its journey. They did not, could not go on without her.

Numbers 20:1–2

The Israelites, the whole congregation, came into the wilderness of Zin in the first month, and the people stayed in Kadesh. Miriam died there, and was buried there.

²Now there was no water for the congregation; so they gathered together against Moses and against Aaron.

The fourth movement is brief. Of the three people Micah would later say together brought Israel out of the house of bondage (Mic. 6:4), Miriam was the first to die. The whole congregation was there.

And of the multitude of that original generation who escaped

Egypt, the multitude that would die in the wilderness because of their faithlessness—Miriam along with Aaron next and Moses last—Miriam alone rates no obituary.[9] Again, it is not so significant that so little is said, though much can be made of that. It is that so little says so much.

God had worked through Miriam to save a baby and through this baby to bring about the deliverance of a people who would change history. Miriam was one of the first to see what God had done and to worship and praise God for what he had done. The leprous Miriam suffered the most physically, perhaps for straying from the path God had set before the people.

And when Miriam died, the whole congregation was there. And in the place Miriam died, there was no water. No Miriam—no water. No Miriam—no life. The water had dried up. It wasn't the first time there was no water, but this time it was especially poignant, and the people despaired. Apparently Aaron and Moses despaired as well, for when they received their instructions to gather the people and to command water from the rock, they expressed their frustration by beating against the rock instead of speaking to it. Miriam was dead; there was no water; and Moses beat against that rock. One wonders what strength Moses derived from Miriam. Without Miriam, Moses whaled against the rock and wailed against God.

The place where Miriam died is the place where Moses and Aaron received their death sentences. When Miriam died, their hope of going over into the Promised Land died too.

Much is said today of how Miriam's story was nearly written out of Scripture, subject to the patriarchal bias of early Hebrew composers. One could easily argue the other way as well, that despite tendencies to leave women nameless and to drop them out of stories altogether, the fact that there are four substantive stories about Miriam may testify to how central she was to the oral tradition of the ancient nation and how determined were subsequent editors to preserve and protect her story. Perhaps Miriam was especially honored.

In one movement Miriam is anonymous. In another, she plays second fiddle. In still another, she receives the full wrath of God. And then she dies.

Taken together, however, we can see how God would not let her song die, how God worked in Miriam and through Miriam to create a vision and to sustain the faith of a wandering people. She could not be drowned out by anyone else's song.

In the first three movements, Miriam's voice is instrumental.

- "Shall I go and get you a nurse from the Hebrew women to nurse the child for you?"
- "Sing to the LORD, for he has triumphed gloriously; horse and rider he has thrown into the sea."
- "Has the LORD spoken only through Moses? Has he not spoken through us also?"

When Miriam is dead and has no voice, the people despair and suffer from thirst.

We cannot hear Miriam's actual speaking voice, and this book is about the actual speaking voice. As we will see in subsequent chapters, however, this book is also about the connection of the voice to the body. *The Symphony of Miriam* is striking in the way her body is involved in each movement. Approaching the Pharaoh's daughter must have been fearsome; dancing must have been exuberant; leprosy must have been deathly frightful; death must have brought relief.

Many will go to the New Testament and the sayings of Paul to make an argument against women using their voices in preaching and leading worship. Some will point out that the twelve disciples chosen by Jesus were all men. But these arguments are obstacles only if taken in isolation.

In 1 Corinthians 14:34, where Paul says that women should keep silent in the church, the larger context often ignored is that Paul was addressing a rather chaotic worshiping situation in Corinth. All of his admonitions in that section of 1 Corinthians have to do with asking the new Christians not to lord their spiritual gifts over one another or to so exercise their freedom in Christ that they drive away unbelievers. More telling than these injunctions is to catch Paul in the act of working with women in ministry. Even in 1 Corinthians, Paul makes note of the ministry of Aquila *and* Prisca and the church in their house (1 Cor. 16:19). In Romans 16, Paul commends Phoebe for her work in the church, and Junia who was in prison with him and was "prominent among the apostles" (Rom. 16:1, 7).

Jesus called twelve disciples at the beginning of his ministry, all men. But we know they were not the only disciples who followed him. Sprinkled throughout the Gospels is evidence that women followed Jesus and provided for him.[10] In the Gospel of John, a woman was the first to see the resurrected Jesus (John 20:11–16). Jesus is an equal-opportunity healer, ministering to women and men alike.

Conclusion

Understanding a biblical view of women and their voices and their right to speak in ministry, even in preaching and the leading of public worship, cannot be had by simply reading *about* women in the Bible. We must catch women *in the act* of speaking and leading in the Bible. This is what we have done with Miriam. This constitutes an inductive and intuitive approach, rather than a deductive and argumentative approach. Even when the argumentative approach is an apologetic for women speaking in the church, it is still one step removed from women actually speaking in the church and witnessing how God works through them and their voices.

From the earliest movements of God's plan of salvation, Miriam was instrumental. That a woman should be so central to the work of God, that a woman's voice should be so central in the lives of God's people, that a woman's body should be so integrally involved in her ministry, is permission-giving to women to be full partners in the ministry of reconciliation. The problem is that not all women feel this permission. Even when ecclesial bodies and local churches grant permission, many women do not exercise their call and right to speak with their voices and bodies.

In the next chapter, we will investigate the signs that women do not have or feel permission to speak and hear the stories of women who have struggled for permission to speak.

CHAPTER 2

Asking Permission

Women who struggle to use their speaking voices in the pulpit usually do not feel they have permission to speak. There are, perhaps, as many reasons for this as there are women who struggle to speak. What these women have in common are the ways in which the lack of permission manifests in their speaking voices. I hear and see the lack of permission in vocal quality, pitch, tone, and volume, in vocal expression, in facial expression, in physical posture, and even in content. Another experience many of these women share is the passion pent up in their bones, their need to preach the gospel. If they didn't have that passion and drive, they would not have been able to overcome the lack of permission enough to speak at all.

A number of stories will be told in this chapter. Some are told by the women themselves in their own voices. Some are about women I have worked with, told from my perspective. The stories are so familiar, so commonplace, that they represent many women with whom I have worked, including women of all ages, from many racial-ethnic identities, and from many Christian faith traditions. When it comes to voices asking permission to speak in the pulpit, it seems no age, no racial-ethnic identity, and no ecclesial tradition is immune.

The stories you will read in this chapter are true and come from women I worked with throughout my teaching ministry at Palmer Theological Seminary in Philadelphia from 1991 to 2001 (then known as the Eastern Baptist Theological Seminary) and at Princeton Theological Seminary from 2001 to the present. In order to protect their privacy, the tellers of the first-person stories have chosen the names under which their stories appear. In terms of issues of abuse, childhood trauma, struggles with gender norms, and ecclesial and cultural discrimination, these stories are not novel. Yet the women who tell their stories here have directly connected their experiences of abuse, trauma, and discrimination with the sound of their own voices. The women who graciously agreed to tell their stories for the purposes of this book each have a unique story; it is their own story. Yet I have found these stories to be paradigmatic. For every story told here, there are dozens more that I have heard from the many women with whom I have worked.

The age and racial, ethnic, and ecclesial identity of the tellers of the three first-person stories is not disclosed. The writing style of each of the first-person narratives was not edited out. There is significance to the author for each word in all capital letters and each quotation mark that becomes in effect an air quote. The stories I tell from my perspective about Korean and African American women are directly related to their racial-ethnic identity. I focus on these two racial-ethnic identities because they represent the largest number of women with whom I have worked who are not Caucasian. While women of all backgrounds may experience the kinds of difficulties expressed by the first-person stories, other dynamics are more specific to racial and ethnic identity and ecclesial tradition. The stories I tell about women who struggled more in the context of their racial and ethnic identities and ecclesial traditions could be considered historical fiction. That is, I see specific women in my mind, but the stories are more an amalgamation of the experiences of many women who bear similar identity and experiences.

These stories are not presented as success stories. Each one of these women is still on a journey, and all would testify that the journey is the thing. Not all vocal problems have been solved; not all contradictory facial expressions have been neutralized; not all wounds have entirely healed; not all psychological and emotional issues have been resolved. But each woman has worked intentionally to claim her voice and her physical space. And she is working still.

Chatty Cathy

Cathy was a mature, second-career seminary student. She was a professional church musician with a family. Her church roots were in a Southern nondenominational fundamentalist tradition. Cathy was a wonderful singer and as a youth participated in traveling evangelistic ministries. Cathy was so effective as a vocalist that she was invited to be lead singer with some nationally renowned ministries. It was always made clear, however, that Cathy would never be able to preach the Word from the pulpit. Women were not allowed to preach.

The first time I heard Cathy preach was in a practicum where the assignment was to preach an Old Testament sermon. Cathy's sermon was on Job. Her written sermon was masterful. Using a parallel construction form of "running the story,"[1] Cathy told contemporary stories as she retold Job's story. Cathy led her hearers into the depth of Job's anguish at the loss of everything in life that pointed to the goodness of God. We felt Job's conflict as he listened to his wife and three would-be friends telling him to repent. Our own righteous indignation rose to meet Job's as he asked, "Where is God?" We found our own personal stories and the situation of our contemporary world in Cathy's sermon. And then she led us into a renewed awareness and apprehension of God's faithfulness.

Her written sermon was masterful; Cathy's identification with human pain and suffering was intense and compassionate; her hearing and explication of the Word was astute and faithful. But Cathy smiled during the entire delivery, using a weak, breathy voice. After the usual post-preaching sermon analysis, I raised the observation that Cathy smiled sweetly during the entire delivery of the sermon. She smiled as she described Job's sores. She smiled as she described the grief that accompanies unbearable loss. She smiled as she reported how Job's friends turned on him. If a hearer did not know what a lovely and compassionate person she is, one would think the smile heartless or perverted or callous. The Germans have a word for it, *schadenfreude*, pleasure that comes at another's misfortune. I also made the observation that for a trained singer, her vocal quality was weak and breathy. The conversation that ensued made it clear that

Cathy was aware of at least the tonal quality issues of her speaking voice. She did not realize she was smiling through the entire sermon. Her early and subsequent professional training in singing gave to smiling the force of habit. She was trained to lift the face and to smile with each inhaled breath. But even more, Cathy's role in ministry in her formative years was to be sweet, to make her hearers feel good, to lift emotions with the power of music, not of speech.

A further complication leading to the ever-present smile was the early training that not only was Cathy forbidden to preach but she could not even participate in the liturgy aside from singing. Each word was a risk; each time she dared to speak in leading worship was a rebellion against what she had known as Christian life and leadership. The sweet smile was a *de facto* apology, an asking of permission to occupy pulpit space. The weak, breathy voice was Cathy's internal conflict about preaching manifesting itself. The power of Cathy's sermon was thoroughly contradicted by her physical posture and vocal quality.

As a professional vocalist, Cathy could be taught not to smile continuously; she could retrain the musculature around her mouth, particularly when she became aware that the smile contradicted what she was saying. The ever-present smile, however, was connected to Cathy's deeply held anxiety and fear that she did not belong in the pulpit. The smile and the light, breathy voice were a means of apologizing to anyone who found her presence in the pulpit offensive. The smile was about more than muscle training. The smile and weak voice were a way of asking permission to be in the pulpit and to say what she had to say. Following is Cathy's story.

Chatty Cathy, in Her Own Words

First there was joy . . . my first memory, that is. I remember being so happy to be alive. I was a little girl reaching for the world with both hands and a wide-open heart . . . happy as a lark. In the morning, I remember the light of the new day penetrating through my closed eyelids like a jolt of electricity. Eyes flying open, my first thought was always, "Oh goody, it's morning! I wonder what I've missed?!" With that, my feet were usually hitting the floor, and I was on my way down the stairs to say good morning to anyone who might be up. Sometimes it was just my mama-kitty, forced to live outside (my mother allowed her into the cellar of our house—but that was it!). So I went outside to say HI!

My parents were young when I was born. I was the oldest child of oldest children who for all intents and purposes were still very much children first and parents second. Both of my parents worked for their respective parents, each family owning their own business. When I was born, my parents had just turned twenty-one, and all of my grandparents were in their early forties. Days and nights were often spent at one or the other grandparents' home.

Being born into such a family was in some ways like having six parents. They were all young and eager to love and shape this next generation, me! My parents and grandparents were all magnificently human, and wonderful, and imperfect. My early "voice" was happy because of my loving reception into this world. My young voice was strong and joy-filled. "Chatty Cathy" was a name affectionately given to me by an indulgent neighbor.

My whole family was full of a zealous faith in Christ. My father's parents were founding members of an independent church, formed by the evangelical fervor that was "crescendoing" during the middle of the twentieth century. My parents met at this church, and we were dyed-in-the-wool "Independents." Church was our second home.

I distinctly remember one Sunday evening, sitting in the "Jewels" Bible class (for children four and five years of age) and being told two important theological concepts that became embedded in my young psyche.

First Message: "God sees you as a precious jewel, and delights in just looking at you and listening to you." I remember straightening my dress and feeling all glow-y and loved. I could almost feel God's eyes warmly adoring me.

Second Message: "God will only be able to hear you if you have told Him everything you have done wrong, all your sins, not leaving one out. If you aren't sure what you've done wrong, ask your parents to help you pray … they'll remember." I remember becoming filled with fear, just sure that I had done so many things wrong that God surely wanted nothing to do with me. Being the hypervigilant firstborn I began trying to work against the odds and transform myself into the "good girl" using all of the mixed messages I received from my parents and grandparents.

The message that had the most profound effect on my life from that day on was about my "VOICE," in the broadest sense of the word. I soon learned that my role was to be a sweet, soft-spoken, helpful to the men, soft-spoken, helpful to everyone, soft-spoken, un-opinionated, good … girl.

So now, I had two strong desires. One desire was to please everyone, and especially to please God. Actually the two things, pleasing everyone and pleasing God, seemed synonymous. Doing it was enormously hard. Being a passionately strong-minded ("high-strung" as my parents put it) and curious little girl, I felt like my very thoughts were offensive to God. I wasn't supposed to be thinking such deep thoughts; men did that, and I was usurping their position. I wasn't supposed to be organizing the neighborhood baseball games; I learned to ask my brothers to do that instead. When I was frustrated or angry, I was supposed to "give it to the Lord" and feel serene peace. If I tried that, and it didn't work, I started to learn that keeping my mouth shut and in the shape of a smile would make others believe I was serene and, most importantly, acceptable.

My God-given voice started to be hushed as I internalized the expectations of many people I loved deeply. I became ashamed of me, sure that my whole self was wrong, and that I needed to let God "reshape" me into the good girl He wished me to be.

The reshaping never really worked. By the time I reached high school, I had become exceedingly helpful and aware that my job was to make everyone within my immediate surroundings happy and peaceful. Sensitized to every angry word or hurt feeling, I would attempt to smooth over any heightened emotion. Never mind that I rarely felt God was close to me, or that He cared about what I felt. I had learned to understand that considering my personal feelings was being selfish, and therefore sinful. I am pretty sure that I was a pressure-cooker of unexpressed emotions, with shame the dominant feeling I experienced.

One thing I can now say I have learned in my life is that God never abandons me, the "real" me, the full-throated toddler who couldn't wait to live. How do I know this?

Going to a very conservative "Bible School" was the next hurdle in my life. It was the only school I was allowed to attend. I was accepted as a sacred music major, but my grandfather told me my real purpose was to get my "M.R.S." degree (wink, wink). I disliked it immediately, thinking the kids around me were insincere and rather odd.

Nearing graduation, I found myself sitting in the pew of a large Catholic cathedral. I challenged God to let me know He was real. I needed to know, or I

*was going to wash my hands of the whole faith thing. After three hours of staring
at the large bronzed crucifix, I calmly got up, relieved. At least I knew now. God
was a creation of mine, not the other way around. I stepped into the busy street
and approached the corner where the old, drunk men tended to gather. I would
always avert my gaze and walked as quickly as I could to avoid the comments
and odors of this cluster of men. This day, something happened that I know now
to be an answer to my prayer in the cathedral. I looked directly at these men, and
God inside of me looked right through me, allowing me to see the world as God
sees it. I felt such incredible, expansive, overwhelming love. I saw these men as
tender, beautiful children, stripped of the layers of crusty pain that life had piled
on to them. I felt an inexpressible tenderness for these men whom I had learned
to disdain. Even the grimy brick wall behind them was glowing with dynamic
light. This was a God-moment. I've never had one like it again.*

*Since then, I have never again questioned the existence of God. Nor have
I questioned the nature of God. Since then, my public life of faith has not been
consistent, due mainly to the many layers of pain that life has piled on to me.
Through the work of many life experiences and many sensitive servants, God has
tenderly exposed the wounds, revealing them for what they are. Then there has
been the bandaging and healing processes, some of them aborted and restarted.*

*Following school, I initially withdrew from "organized religion," feeling
confusion at the experience of God I had received on the street corner versus the
experience of God I had received in the church. I remember the day when a Presbyterian pastor said to me, "Cathy, I would like to pray for the pain that you've
received at the hands of the church." A window was thrown open for God's Spirit
to fly through into my heart. Some of the shame was replaced by true peace.*

*Eventually I began working within the church as a musician. As often hap-
pens, God heals us in the middle of our work, not before we begin. And of course,
healing is never completed; it is a progression. I've learned to see everyone within
the wider world, and particularly in the church, as God's "work-in-process."*

*As I've been able to receive more and more of God's grace in my life, I also
have become more and more restored to my authentic "self." This journey of restoration eventually took me to seminary. There I found that my passionate and
inquisitive nature is a gift from God, not a sin. It was from wonderful professors
that I was given "faith handles," which I understand as the permission, the space,
and the time to develop my own personal expression of my walk with God. I
learned it is OK for even a "good girl" to question and struggle, to get angry, and*

most importantly, to be heard. Seminary was a place where God struggled with me as I read hundreds of books on other people's conclusions about God. All the time, God was calling me deeper into relationship so that I began to distill the things that are features of my personal faith story.

It was not easy speaking with authority, or even comfort, about God. One day, in my third preaching class, I delivered a sermon about the "Sovereignty of God." I had already received an "A" on content for this sermon in another class, so I was thinking it would be a hit. Not so. It was the delivery that did not receive an "A" on that day. I will never forget my professor saying lovingly but firmly to me as I finished, "Cathy, you are a singer. Why don't you know how to use your voice when you speak? By the way, don't you ever put final consonants on words? One more thing, did you really mean to smile when you said 'over 10,000 were killed in Bosnia'?"

Taking the video of my sovereignty sermon, I quickly drove home to see what she was talking about. Several minutes into the video, I had to turn it off. I knew exactly what she meant. I felt God saying to me, "You know how to speak in front of people. Just do it." The words were not audible, but I knew it was God asking me to step up and turn my back on my fear. I knew I had the God-given tools; I just never thought I was supposed to use them. I suddenly knew I would be unfaithful to God if I didn't, something about "putting my light under a bushel."

Since that time, I have graduated from seminary, and I increasingly have opportunities to preach and serve others in ministry. I understand now that God let me see through "God-eyes" back there on that city street so that I could boldly speak of a God who loves us all beyond our imaginations. God equipped me with a "voice" at birth to say that very thing.

I understand now that God loves me, and it has nothing to do with me getting anything right. Although I keep trying, it is clear that I only get it right when I stay painstakingly honest and sincerely humble before God and others. I know now that God loves me, and always has. I think I came into the world knowing that and responding with love to God and the Creation. My original voice was, and is, my true "VOICE." My prayer to my life's end is for the grace to continue speaking authentically, increasingly using the "voice" God created.

Sarah

When Sarah came to my speech class, she made it clear to me that this was an enormously paralyzing experience. She had already failed the required speech course once, unable to stand before the class and speak a word without immediately bursting into tears. I assured her that we would start with where she was and go slowly, I wouldn't push her, and that the environment created would be safe.

One of our first exercises was to stand in a large circle, not close together but with plenty of space between people. There were eight students in the section. We would read through some simple vocal exercises designed to experiment with the sound of our own voices. We went around the circle. No eye contact was needed; it was simply an exercise in vocal play. Sarah's voice was predictably small and weak, but that is not what struck me. What struck me was Sarah's physical posture. She was standing three people to my right and had assumed a posture of defense, turning her body from me and hunching her left shoulder as if to protect her head. What struck me was that Sarah looked as if she expected to be struck. Over time, I came to learn that Sarah's fear of speaking was profoundly deep and deeply rooted in difficult childhood and adolescent circumstances that were not entirely relieved or resolved as she entered adulthood. Her disconnect from her body was so pronounced that she could hardly speak at all. This was only the beginning of my journey with Sarah. Her journey had begun years before. Following is Sarah's story.

Sarah, in Her Own Words

As a little girl, I loved the sound of my own voice. I lectured my dolls, babbled on my play telephone, and sang at the top of my lungs. I sat under the maple tree in the front yard and yodeled for hours. My voice could make the hallway walls echo, the sparklies on the chandelier quiver, and the family dog jump. My voice made the boy next door let go of my hair when I screamed NO! in his ear, and it made my friend give me back my doll when I yelled YES! It made the teacher call my name when I shouted ME! ME! At night my voice kept me company as I whispered my prayers in the dark.

How do little girls lose their voices? When I went to church and the men had the microphones while the women prayed silently with eyes down, I learned a woman's voice wasn't worthy to be heard by men or by God. When the preacher said that Eve's mouth had brought sin into the world when she spoke temptation to Adam with the apple, which stood for sex, I learned that being in a girl body was wrong, evil, dangerous, and that using a female voice could be catastrophic, could cause the Fall of all Mankind. When boys got called on in class over and over while I waved my hand frantically to answer, I learned what girls said didn't count. When I was hit, I learned not to cry out; no one would help me anyway, and my tears only led to more rage and more blows. When I was molested, I learned to swallow my no, to let go of what I wanted and what was rightfully mine. I learned that telling anyone what I had experienced could be catastrophic; he said it would be, and I believed him, because women were bad, and men were always right, and Adam had eaten the apple. My own lived experience began to be alienated from me, my own body a numb blank, my own thoughts a repetitive loop of nonsense that allowed me to avoid thinking about anything dangerous, which came to include what had happened to me, how my body felt, and the fact that I actually existed. I pretended most of the time that I did not exist. At night, where there used to be prayer, there was only silence.

At puberty when my walk started to shift and my voice dropped, I learned that boys like girls who talk in high, squeaky voices and giggle a lot, and grownups like girls who don't talk at all and smile a lot, and girls don't like other girls, no matter how they talk. So I sucked in my words and stopped talking, sucked in my stomach and stopped breathing. My shoulders rode up next to my ears; I took little steps so not to wiggle when I walked; and I smiled a lot, not a wide open-mouthed grin but a little close-mouthed smirk to show restraint, self-control, modesty. I wanted to show that I was fine, just fine! I didn't want my body to tell on me. I didn't want to have a body at all. I didn't want to cause any trouble. I wanted to be a good girl, invisible, silent, sweet. Shh.

How did I find my voice again? I found it by trying to speak the Word of God. When I went to college, I studied art, and found myself sitting in the dark staring at slides of crucifixes, Madonnas, and illuminated Gospel pages. These images spoke to me. There was color, beauty, meaning in Christianity that I hadn't been aware of, and Christianity was much older and deeper than the religion of my childhood had led me to believe. I felt I should not give up on my faith. I found a church tradition that was open to women in leadership, with a more holistic theology and a different relationship to Scripture and history. I fell in love with the beauty and truth of the Word as it was preached at that church. I began teaching children's Sunday school, then led a small group. I began to want to share with others the good news that I had first heard in my childhood church and that I had finally embraced in my new church. I began to consider the possibility of a life in ministry. Others saw in me gifts for pastoral leadership, but it was hard to see myself as a preacher. Still, I wanted to become what I felt called to be, and I hoped God would change and equip me on the way.

It was not an easy change. In speech class at seminary, I stood at the podium and couldn't speak. Breathe, said the teacher. We can't hear you, said the class. Be present with us, said the teacher. We can just barely hear you, said the class. How about stepping forward as you make that point? said the teacher. Ok, said the teacher, let's try again tomorrow. If I was going to speak God's Word, first I would have to learn to speak.

I went home and looked in the mirror and watched myself breathe. My chest didn't move; my belly didn't move. It was as if I was holding my breath, bracing for the next bad thing to happen. And I couldn't feel anything, from the inside, from the neck down. I prayed, for the first time in a long time, for help. And for the first time in a long time, I got an answer. I went to hula dancing class. I stood in the back of the class for three months before I could move my left foot six inches forward and let my body follow it through space, before I could shift my weight in my hips, and it was over a year before I could join in the closing song at the end of the class.

In the meantime, I met one-on-one with the speech teacher, gripping my paper. Breathe, stand your ground, release the large muscles, said the teacher. How do I breathe? When the belly is expanding, you are inhaling, said the teacher. I did not want my belly to expand, let alone to notice it expanding. I did not want to have a belly at all. But I wanted to learn to speak. I felt it was now or never; I felt God was calling me to speak; and I had begun to revise the crazy-making theology of my upbringing. With practice, having an expanding belly became tolerable, first alone, then one-on-one, then in class. Moment by moment I began to be willing to inhabit my body, to experience it, to be it, even though at first all I experienced was tension, muscle pain, and adrenalin, and I felt as awkward as an orangutan in a tutu. I had to be willing to be present, to be seen, to exist, *and take up space, to let myself be who I was, know what I knew, feel what I felt. That had a cost: I had to reckon with evil, with pain, with my own vulnerable humanity, and with all that I had lost as a result of the abuse and how it shaped my choices, as a result of the warped theology I grew up with and accepted, and as a result of simply being female in a culture where that is seen as a problem, a challenge, a risk, a threat. But slowly, sometimes, I was able to speak. I found some words to try out, and the class clapped when I sat down. We could hear you this time! said the class. We'll work on eye contact later, said the teacher.*

I started singing again, in the car at first, softly with a very loud radio on. I started lecturing, a few words at a time, to my dog, about how girls have just as much right as boys to laugh and sing, and how women have as much right as men to stand and speak. I started humming, very quietly, when I sat out under a tree. I started telling, a little at a time, my story, and no one struck me dead. And I danced.

And I talk now, on the phone, and I sing now, in church, and anywhere, and I can make the walls echo and the chandelier quiver and make anybody jump, if I have to. My voice is lower now, and that's useful, and I can squeal if I feel like it, and that's fun. I can feel my belly from the inside out, and my breath goes all the way in and out. These days I hear myself, a whispering singing shouting yodeling demanding lecturing praying woman, and I hear myself say, Ouch, No, Yes, Me! Me! And I hear myself say Jesus, and grace, and thanks. I hear myself say, Amen. I hear my voice, coming from my body, and it is me.

Christine

Christine was a capable and competent speaker when she came to my workshop. She was an every-Sunday preacher for whom ministry was a second career. It was an intensive workshop, and the women who were there had chosen to be there; this was not a required course. In such a context, there is not a lot of time to work slowly into the task at hand. I made the early observation that Christine's pitch range was low and narrow. I was certain she was at the bottom of her pitch range even though I had never met or heard her before. The telling signs were running out of air prematurely and a glottal fry, a gravelly phonation at the bottom of the pitch range that is frequently present at the end of phrases as air runs out.

What I did not know was that I had struck a nerve. Christine's reaction was immediate. She had no problem telling the group that she had been severely criticized by a supervisor at work when she started her first career. This supervisor was a woman who did not seem to have Christine's best interests in mind; rather, it seems the supervisor was threatened by Christine. Christine's experience highlights one that is not infrequent: the harshest criticism might come from other women. There is a sense in which men can afford to be more gracious, even if that is a patronizing graciousness; they are not threatened by the women around them, especially when they are in charge of the patriarchal system that is keeping women in their place. It is harder for women to be noticed; harder for women to be rewarded for their good work; more likely for the promotion of a woman to be a token promotion. Women, therefore, sometimes pose a greater threat to other women.

Another dimension of Christine's story is that she linked her voice to her personhood. When her voice was criticized, she felt cut to the core. She came at it from a different direction than Chatty Cathy and Sarah, but they testify to the same thing: their voices, produced by their bodies, are integral to who they are. That Christine's personhood became an issue in the workplace is not unusual. A woman's work performance is often evaluated not only on what she does, but also on what she wears, how she carries herself, and how her voice sounds: on who she is. This can lead to the extreme self-consciousness that Christine experienced as an obstacle to using her voice.

A third dimension Christine observes is the impact a woman's fluctuating hormones have on her voice. We will explore this further in chapter 4. The impact of menstrual cycling is not so great that others would notice. But it can be felt and heard by a woman who knows she does not have a cold, or she did not stress her voice celebrating at a party or a ballgame, or that she did not consume alcohol the night before—all conditions that can lead to a negative impact on the voice, and to self-consciousness. That negative impact is usually a compromised pitch range—the higher pitches are not available to the woman—or throatiness or sounding congested. Following is Christine's story.

Christine, in Her Own Words

I have had a complicated relationship with my voice from a young age. I didn't know there was a problem with my voice until I was in grade three and my report card came home with the notation, "Christine can't sing in tune." I became completely paranoid about my singing voice and was shy to "sing out loud." None of my music teachers ever talked about how to learn to sing so that I could improve. It was just, "Christine can't sing in tune." This was heartbreaking for me because I loved to sing and wanted to sing.

While using my singing voice was challenging, I excelled at public speaking. Each year we had to research a topic of interest and write and present a speech. I loved doing this! The winner of the classroom competition went to the school competition, and the winner of the school competition went to the Legion. I went to the Legion several years and placed well. I worked on memorizing and using cue cards and public speaking techniques. I received praise for this, so it never occurred to me that my speaking voice was a problem. I also participated in the annual theatrical productions in school. I generally had a lead role, so at least my voice in public speaking was affirmed.

It was when I started my first career after college that I was told there was a problem with my speaking voice. My first boss was controlling, opinionated, and, frankly, a mean woman. Rather than supporting others and trying to build them up, she would criticize and tear them down. She frequently told me that she didn't like my voice. She thought it was too high and told me I should lower it. This wasn't phrased as helpful or constructive criticism but as though she was disgusted, as though she was repulsed by my voice. I had to change it.

For the first time, I became very self-conscious about my speaking voice. I worked to try to control it and make it lower. This resulted in my voice becoming more monotone, especially when I was aware of being watched or that I was being heard by many people, such as when making presentations, or when changing my voicemail greeting every day. When I was relaxed, my voice was more "normal."

As I was more aware of my voice and could hear my boss's criticism in my head, I was aware that it sounded tight and strained when I was nervous. This bothered me, and I became very self-conscious about it. I tried even harder to control it, and it became flatter, with less range.

As I began seminary and began to lead worship, I was nervous because I did it infrequently. I was nervous because I was proclaiming God's Word and felt inadequate to do so. I was nervous because I had already been criticized for my voice, and I became aware of how vulnerable we are when we lead worship. We're exposed, and people are evaluating us for such things as the way we lead, for our theology, and for the way we say things. I had one friend who happened to be a musician say to me after one of my first sermons that my voice range was small.

One odd thing I have noticed over the years, in seminary and beyond, is that the quality of my voice changes as I approach the time of getting my period. Is there a physiological connection? Sometimes this was the clue that my period was coming. I would notice my voice, look at the calendar, and sure enough, the timing of my menstrual cycle lined up with the change in my voice. My period was coming.

Before I moved to my current call, I took voice and singing lessons for two years from someone who specialized in voice pedagogy and taught in the music school at university. This was a huge confidence booster—I could sing! We also worked on my range and breathing. I have been feeling lately like I need— or want—to take voice lessons again as my confidence in my singing voice is diminishing.

I've been preaching weekly for more than three years now. Most of the time, I don't get nervous about my voice. I'm aware of what it's like when it's tight, but that happens much less frequently. I am starting to listen to the worship services I lead as a way of evaluating and reflecting on my voice. It becomes easier with time, but at first I had to force myself to do so. It helps to be able to reflect upon how you think you are creating meaning and emphasis, and then hear what is actually coming out. I'm aware of what I eat and drink before I lead worship. Alcohol and milk products the night before public speaking are not helpful. I'm also aware of the need for rest.

I feel so called to ministry, to proclaim God's Word and share the love of Jesus, and I believe God called me as I am. God gave me this voice. I'm trying to work on this tool just as I'm trying to evolve in my preaching style to become more effective. I'm aware of it now when I'm trying to control my voice too much, when I fall into the old habit of making it monotone. My speaking is more effective when I'm not trying to control my voice.

Given the love/hate relationship I've had with my voice, I find it ironic that I'm in a vocation that is so dependent upon my voice. The pain of what my former boss said about my voice has been very real, and the wounds deep and hard to heal. The criticism was painful because she wasn't just saying I needed to become better at x, y, or z but that there was something wrong with me, my personhood. Her criticism cut to my core and a place where I was already feeling vulnerable. Power was very important to her, and she was the type of person who wanted everything done her way. The harm she did to me, my confidence, my sense of self-worth, and my ability to see and appreciate the gifts I have was severe. She held a lot of power over me and chose to misuse it. What if she would have chosen to be a mentor? Perhaps this is what she thought she was doing. I also have to take responsibility for staying in that role, under her supervision, for so long. In some ways, it feels like she "broke me," and I needed other people and experiences to help me see myself differently.

As I write, I once again realize just how complicated my relationship is with my voice. The old ghosts continue to reappear. Just recently I was meeting with the music director and noticed my voice was "scratchy." Most people would write this off as a bad day, or having a frog in their throat. But I was thinking about how my voice is letting me down, and I was worried about what the other person was thinking—the music director, no less!

Gi

Gi is the name I have given to the Korean women about whom I speak in this section. Gi means "brave one." Gi came to me as a seminary graduate who by her own admission had not focused well on her speech classes. Speech classes are very difficult for students for whom English is a second language. They have to focus so hard on comprehension, vocabulary, and composition in academics that the way they use the voice in speaking or oral interpretation in English is not the primary concern. Like many Korean women who have no vision for ordained ministry, since it is prohibited in their particular tradition, Gi began seminary in a Master of Arts program.[2] She did not expect to be ordained, and did not expect to complete a Master of Divinity degree. Only later did she acknowledge her call to ordained ministry and finish a Master of Divinity degree. It was after her ordination in a mainline denomination that Gi came to me, realizing that the only way she would be allowed to be a preacher was to become the pastor of an Anglo congregation—or of an English-speaking church.

Gi was an adult immigrant to the United States. Her spoken English was not strong, nor were her worship leadership skills. Gi knew she needed help; she had no idea how to become a worship leader because she had never envisioned herself becoming one.

At our first meeting, what I call a diagnostic conference, I gave Gi material to prepare for our first work session. I gave her a call to worship that she needed to learn and deliver at our next meeting. Essentially it was a short Scripture passage that was chosen for the rhetorical purpose of a solo call to worship. When we met again, I told Gi to go up to the front of the room, sit in the chair as if she had just entered the sanctuary and was waiting for the prelude to end, and then go to the lectern and deliver the call to worship. Gi went to the front of the room and sat down. I announced that the prelude had just ended and gestured to her to approach the lectern. She then asked me if she should stand. We started again. I explained that when I announced the end of the prelude, the opening music, she should stand and approach the lectern. Several tries later, after repeatedly asking me if she should stand—in essence asking permission to stand—Gi stood on cue and approached the lectern. She looked at her notes, looked at me, looked at her notes, looked at me, looked at her notes again, and finally looked at me and asked if she should start. I clarified that I was the congregation, and she should not ask the congregation for permission to start. In our workshop setting, the call to worship comes directly at the end of the prelude. So she should stand and approach the lectern at the end of the prelude, set her notes, look up to the congregation, and begin.

We did this exercise several times that day before Gi could approach the lectern and simply begin the call to worship without directly asking permission to speak. Her respect for me in my position as teacher, her uncertainty of her own authority, and her complete inability to envision herself in this role were paralyzing. And she would begin ministry in her own church within months. Gi told me her story.

When Gi was a young girl, she had a loud, playful, joyful voice. She loved to sing and laugh. She was unself-conscious and unrestrained as she played. As she got a bit older, the neighbors began to complain. Gi lived in an apartment building where the sounds from one apartment and one floor traveled easily to the next. The neighbors complained that Gi was too loud. Her mother told her to lower her voice. Lowering her voice did not come easily or naturally to Gi, however, so she had to be corrected many times. Finally, the neighbors threatened more drastic measures, and Gi's mother told her that they would suffer a natural disaster and the apartment building would be destroyed if she did not restrain herself, lower the volume of her voice, and studiously avoid being heard by anyone outside their own apartment.

Gi learned that it was literally dangerous to freely exercise the use of her voice. She learned to speak in quiet and submissive tones. Many Korean women like Gi have told me that in a traditional Korean context, the volume of the voice is determined by whether there are men in the room. The woman's voice must never be louder than the men's voices in the same space. Furthermore, the Korean language employs a complex system of grammatical constructions that indicates the relationship of the speaker to the hearer. Speakers use an extensive number of words or titles that denote members of the family, with each word being determined by the position of the person within the family. By using these particular words in the subject of the speech, and by using particular word endings and sentence endings, a speaker declares her place in relation to the hearer and the object of her speech. This aspect of the Korean language is referred to as "honorifics," or what some call "polite speech."

In the larger American English-speaking context, for example, we would use the terms "aunt" and "uncle" for everyone who is a brother or sister of our parents, and perhaps even for close family friends. In the Korean language, specific words for aunt and uncle indicate the place of the person in the family in order of age. The age of the speaker, the gender, the familial or social relationship of the speaker to the hearer, and even the content of speech are all deftly taken into account by the traditionally competent speaker of the Korean language.[3]

Some scholars and speakers of the language equate honorifics with politeness: when proper honorifics are being used, a person is being polite. Not everyone agrees. One scholar suggests three rules of politeness in Korean speech: (1) don't impose; (2) give options; and (3) make a person feel good—be friendly.[4] These are dimensions of politeness in Korean speech that go beyond particular titles, word endings, and sentence construction. The use of honorifics and dimensions of polite speech are second nature to the native Korean speaker and are learned in some measure by American-born Koreans for whom Korean is the first language spoken in the home.

There are also levels of honorifics, from the most respectful in the most formal context to the least formal in language used between close friends or spouses. The number of levels of honorifics is also a subject of debate. It is not for me to comment on the scholarly disputes over whether there are three levels of honorifics in traditional Korean language, or six, or some number in between. I am in no position to comment on the differences, if there are any, between honorifics and politeness. But what strikes me is that women who come from some level of traditional Korean culture, even if they were born in the United States, have a tremendous amount of cultural complexity to navigate as they move in and out of typical American English-speaking culture, especially in mixed audiences along the spectrum of traditional Korean to more traditional "American." It is possible that my exhortation to create more sound, and the desire of congregations that their women pastors create more sound, might be so counter to how these women have been raised that it is not only difficult for them, it might be downright offensive to them.

There does seem to be one caveat, however. One scholar suggests that while politeness might mean softening illocutionary force, it might be the case that the propositional content of the speech requires greater illocutionary force in order to be polite.[5] From this I would suggest that the role of preaching and leading in worship, and even the role of teaching a Bible study where men are present, are contexts in which the woman speaker is entitled to more "illocutionary force." I take illocutionary force to mean speaking with greater volume, more pronounced diction, and even with a more forceful tone as a way to convey the speaker's conviction.

Some Korean women have told me that, when speaking English, they are relieved to be free of the system of Korean honorifics. I know there are those who are not entirely free of the cultural imprint, however, when I see and hear how hard it is for some women raised in a traditional Korean culture to make a sound loud enough for everyone in the room to hear.

Atara

Atara is the name I have given to the African American women about whom I speak in this section. Atara is a Hebrew name that means "diadem," a crown worn by royalty. In my mind, Atara is a regal one.

Atara grew up in a major city in the United States. She came from a family of strong women and a father who was her rock, especially when her mother died while Atara was still a young woman. Atara enjoyed singing in a church choir in a multiracial congregation, but she had no vision, not even a notion of ministry, until a white pastor of the congregation pulled her aside and told her she had a call to vocational ministry and she should pursue that call. A woman minister did not fit with Atara's image of the church. She did not know what "seminary" was. Her response was, "What's a call?"

A common problem among many of my African American female students is that they have not experienced permission to preach from the pulpits of their own churches. Some did not have permission even to identify the longing in their hearts as a call to preach. Some came to seminary in order to prepare for non-preaching ministries: evangelism, missions, women's ministries, and educational ministries, though most, in my experience, wanted to preach and held out hope to one day have a preaching ministry. It was a significant accomplishment, however, to receive approval from the men in their lives, their pastors and husbands, to come to seminary. For some, being allowed to come to seminary at all was a sign of being progressive.

Some women, like Atara, had no idea what a call was. Black church preaching traditions are very strong, and while there are traditions that embrace women ministers and preachers, such as the American and Progressive Baptist churches and some expressions of Pentecostalism, there are still those who do not. Nevertheless, the gospel is so strongly preached in these traditions that they cannot help but raise up women preachers. The Spirit works as the Spirit will.

Atara began to listen to herself and to ask God what God wanted for her life. She already had a profession, and having been a teenage mother, was already caring for one child. She realized God was nudging her forward, somewhere, and began a long commute on weekends for part-time seminary studies. Atara did not know where seminary was leading her—she still had no vision for ministry—and she did not know her own self, her own Voice, nor did she trust herself. She subsequently married a man who she thought would be her helpmate and would protect her, a man who would complement her own way in the world.

Atara moved so that she could attend seminary at a traditionally black school. It was in a pastoral counseling class where the professor was describing the dynamics of domestic abuse that it dawned on Atara that he was describing her life. Subtle beginnings as emotional and psychological abuse by her husband had recently become physical. Atara came to realize that if she stayed in the relationship, she would die. She also came to realize that while she thought she was going to seminary to learn about God, she was actually discovering herself for the first time.

Not only did Atara not have a Voice, an identity of her own, or a voice, she did not know until she was in seminary that anything was missing. When she realized she was the victim of abuse, still a victim and not yet a survivor as she puts it, she began to talk about it. She went to a support group for victims and survivors of abuse and talked about her experience. She exercised her voice to challenge the cultural undercurrents that had made it difficult for her to recognize she was a victim of domestic abuse. She used her voice to challenge those who would "use the Bible as a belt," including the woman who, knowing she had been abused, told her divorce was a sin. She gained clarity about the positive aspects of her upbringing as an African American woman, having been raised to be nurturing and forgiving, to be the strong one, to help, save, deliver, and bear life. She also realized that these positive aspects of her upbringing did not require her to sacrifice herself. She gained clarity that taking care of the family did not have to mean neglecting herself. She learned that no matter how hard she worked or how hard she prayed or how long she stayed with her abusive husband, she might not be able "to bring him into the marvelous light." Most of all, she learned that to be truly gracious to another, she had to allow God to be gracious to her. And that grace meant she did not have to remain silent or in an abusive relationship.

It was realizing she was in an abusive relationship that woke Atara up. In her awakening, she discovered who she is, that she has an identity, and that she has a voice she can use to bear truthful witness to the gospel. The awakening and the circumstances of the awakening to one's own voice do not have to be so dramatic, and they certainly do not have to include an abusive relationship. Another of my students, from a black Baptist tradition, struggled to use her voice in classroom preaching even though she said she had the support of her pastor and home church. She told me one day that she had decided to transfer her membership to another church in the same city, claiming she was doing this for reasons concerning theology and worship style, not because of a lack of support from the first pastor. Only after extended conversation did it surface that the first pastor never let her preach or lead in worship. She came from a tradition where those who are "anointed" may begin preaching at a young age and certainly before any formal theological training. She was recognized as such a person by the pastor, but she never received an opportunity to preach even though the men who were so recognized did preach. The pastor did not rally the support of the congregation for this woman. He verbalized support to her personally and privately, but indicated with his actions in public quite the opposite. She finally had to admit to herself that she was not receiving the support she needed and went to a church that embraced her call. I never did figure out if her reluctance to tell me she was not allowed to preach in her home church was a source of embarrassment, or a reality that she just did not want to admit. These are painful realizations. We want to think that those whom we love and respect will support us. So long as there are local and ecclesial traditions that do not recognize fully the God-given gifts and rights of women to be full partners in ministry, many women will receive the message that it is not permissible for them to preach the gospel.

Still other African American women have talked about the difficulty of finding their own voices when all they have heard are male preachers. In traditions where preaching is caught as much as taught, where one learns to preach in part by imitation, having only male preachers to imitate can lead to a woman feeling inauthentic.

Atara is now ordained in a historically African American tradition that has women preachers; however, they are still too few and far between. Atara sees accomplished women serving in all aspects of the church, not only in roles such as secretary and ushers, hospitality and nurturers of children, but in leadership and governing roles. Nevertheless, from her perspective, and it is not unfounded, it is still the men who seem to control who will be in the pulpit.[6]

Conclusion

The difficulties many women have to overcome in order to use their voices to preach the gospel are fairly dramatic, but not all are. As I said at the beginning of this chapter, there are probably as many stories as there are women who struggle to preach. The stories in this chapter have been representative of my experience with women during my teaching years. In some cases, women have to leave their home communities and seek out new communities of faith where their voices will be accepted and heard. Often, however, with increased understanding comes mutual efforts to overcome historic barriers. Once again, the connection of the voice to the body and the body to self-understanding is critical.

In the next chapter, we will look more closely at why women are disconnected from their bodies.

CHAPTER 3

Voice Lost

My denomination, what is now the Presbyterian Church (USA), began ordaining women in the year of my birth, 1956. Nevertheless, I never saw a woman serving as pastor while growing up. When I was in college I heard rumors of a female pastor in a nearby Methodist church, and one young woman from my home congregation began seminary studies. She interned at our home church, and when I was home on vacation, I saw her lead worship. I met my first female ordained Presbyterian minister at seminary.

When I began seminary in 1978, although the denomination had been ordaining women for twenty-two years, the issue of the ordination of women was not at all settled in the church. Many of my interviews during my senior year, interviews for positions as assistant pastor for youth and/or Christian education, were clearly token interviews. The churches needed to be able to say that they had considered female candidates, but many had no intention of calling a woman as pastor. It was fairly easy for my female colleagues and me to discern when we were in a token interview. Some of us were angered by this; many of us continued with such interviews for the practice and on the premise that we just might change someone's mind.

My golden interview moment of that season came at the home of a search committee member after a full day of meetings at the church and dinner out with the committee. This was clearly not a token interview; I was a candidate for the position. We were in the formal interview with the committee over dessert. It seemed this church was very serious about me, and I could easily see myself on staff at this church. We were getting along famously when one of the women began to hem and haw, and finally blurted out her question, "Do you like boys?" This was the spring of 1981, and recent actions of the General Assembly of the then UPC(USA), now the PC(USA), regarding the "definitive guidance" governing the non-ordination of self-avowed, practicing homosexuals was still being hotly debated. "Do you like boys?" The room froze. They knew I was not married. They knew I was a "traditional student": straight through college to seminary and straight through seminary, which put me at about twenty-five years old. They knew my basic demographic. Here I was going into a traditionally male vocation. Boys? *Boys?!* What was she asking? She was not allowed to ask if I was gay. It happens I am not (which would have been the right answer), but she was not allowed to ask! Was the question a reflection of my appearance? Did I not look feminine enough? I was an athlete, a swimmer, broad shouldered—I had even been told by the head resident of my dorm in college that I looked like a linebacker. Do I like *boys?* I tried so hard to hit the dress code just right: business-like, professional, not severe, still feminine. Did I miss the mark? Was it something I said? Was it my short hair? It wasn't *that* short! The hush over the room felt like an eternity while my mind searched for the appropriate response. "You are not allowed to ask that question!" would have been an appropriate response for me. Direct. Clear. That is what I felt. That is what I knew. But I also felt that such a direct response would be impolite; it wasn't nice! I had the right to say NO. I felt NO deep in my gut: NO, not in answer to the question, but NO to the idea of even asking the question. But I did not feel permission to say the NO.

Maybe she did not know she wasn't allowed to ask that question. I did not want to embarrass her. (I did not want to embarrass *her!*) You could have heard a pin drop on the carpet while all eyes were on me. I did not want to embarrass her because I did not want to be rude; I wanted to be nice. I did not want to embarrass her because if I was too direct, perhaps my candidacy would be over. Maybe I should self-declare my candidacy over. No one else in the room was speaking up. Maybe they were all secretly wondering if "I liked boys"—whatever that meant. All of these thoughts raced through my head in a matter of seconds. Finally I did what I have always tended to do in awkward moments; I deflected with humor. "Yes, as a matter of fact, I do like boys. But I prefer *men.*" The room cracked up. People practically slapped their knees in relieved laughter, and only then did some of them turn to her and say, "You can't ask that question!" Of course, they waited for me to answer before correcting her.

When finally some sense of order fell back upon the room, the woman clarified that I would be working with junior high boys, and not "everyone" (read "girls") can get along with junior high boys. Could I manage junior high boys? Could I get down on the floor and wrestle and rough house with them and handle their sometimes unruly behavior? There are so many things wrong with those questions it is hardly worth going into here. But would a committee member have asked a twenty-five-year-old unmarried man if he liked girls? Or would they all have been thinking about the eligible "girls" they would introduce to him? And would the average man have gone through all the mental gymnastics I went through to craft an answer that connected my gut, what I knew to be true, with the need to be nice and not to embarrass anyone?

I did not receive a call to that church, and went on to serve elsewhere. My generation, including those who came several years before me, began to populate the churches with women pastors. Most of us were probably in staff positions, but we were there. When I began teaching seminary ten years later, many of my female students had had women as pastors. Not only had they grown up with the idea of women as pastors, but they had been nurtured by them. I was under the impression that once given ecclesial permission and the opportunity to change the culture in local churches, women would come to the business of public worship leadership with a confidence that many of my classmates did not have. However, I have found this generally not to be the case.

I wondered for years why women who had received support from their denominations, from their home churches, and from their pastors still preached and conducted worship with such meekness. I wondered why women who had permission to speak up did

not speak up. Why did women who did not need to fight these battles diminish themselves physically? Why did so many look like
they wanted *physically* to cave in upon themselves? What were they
hiding from? What were they apologizing for? Why couldn't they
claim their physical space in the pulpit? If their call to ministry had
been embraced and affirmed, especially at the local level, why did
so many of my female students continue to speak with such tiny
voices?

One answer, of course, is that not all of these women had received
unqualified support. As I learned from the experience of Atara and
other women in chapter 2, women can receive mixed messages from
their churches regarding the call to preach. Denominational policy
might affirm and support women's ordination and women in the
pulpit, but in local practice you might never actually find a woman
in the pulpit.

Nevertheless, with so much progress being made and many
women receiving full support, why did they have such trouble using
their voices? Why did my women who were affirmed in their call to
the gospel ministry struggle to speak?

Talking Heads

In my speech classes, we begin by learning how to use the physical
voice. In order to use the voice, women must feel that it is theirs
to use; they must own it. And to own it, they need to know what
it is and how it works. I explain to my students that the voice is a
full-body instrument. It starts with a base of support at the feet. I
often liken the body's use in vocal production to a grand piano. The
concert grand piano is connected to the floor. It is connected to a
wood floor. The wooden stage floor on which a concert grand sits is
an extension of the piano. You don't see a grand piano in a concert
setting on a carpeted floor. The piano actually gains resonance from
the floor. Or consider a true mechanical wooden music box. Hold
the music box in the air while playing it, and there will be a small,
even tinny sound, as the teeth of a steel comb strike the pins on a

brass cylinder. Place the music box on a wooden table, and listen to the full and loud resonance when the table becomes an extension of the sound.

The resonance of our voices is dependent upon a firm base of support that begins with our feet fully connected to the floor. The best way to experience this is to walk around barefoot, noticing the connection of the feet to the floor, paying attention to what it feels like to have this base of support. This base is so important that women will find it more difficult to use their voices effectively if they are wearing very high heels or thin, pointy, stiletto heels. Even if one is accustomed to wearing these shoes, wearing them does not promote good vocal production. The voice is a full-body instrument and relies on the use of the full body from foot to head for full and resonant production.

The problem I came to see was that many of my women were disconnected from their bodies. They were talking heads. I compare it to taking the mouthpiece off of a wind instrument and buzzing (in the case of a brass instrument), or honking/squeaking (in the case of a reed instrument), and trying to make it sound like the horn is fully attached. There is no way the mouthpiece alone can replicate the sound. Typically my women have had trouble connecting the mouthpiece, the head, to the full body of the horn, the instrument—their bodies. Their bodies do not cooperate with what their mind is telling them to do. No matter how I suggest they arrange their bodies, they have trouble getting their bodies to follow. They struggle to assume a stance with their feet more than a couple of inches apart or with their weight evenly distributed upon both feet. Usually their feet and legs are placed tightly together in the way most women are taught to stand. Shoulders are often caved in, and elbows cling tightly to their sides. Not infrequently the head is cocked to one side or the other in a rather cute pose that suggests the question, "Is it all right with you if I stand here and speak?"

It became clear that correcting the stance did not correct the problem, because the head and the body were in conflict and were not working together harmoniously. The head and heart wanted to speak, but the body said no or the body was afraid; the body did not want to follow. On the other hand, I sometimes had the sense that, even when the body was in the ideal speaking posture and appeared ready to speak, the mind and heart appeared to have vacated the premises, perhaps out of fear or shame. Arranging the body in an ideal posture for speaking was so threatening that the head and heart no longer wanted to speak. The women struggled to inhabit a grounded, open body. Ultimately, these women had disconnected their thoughts and feelings from their bodies and bodily expression. They were disconnected from their bodies, so they could not use their voices effectively.

What does this disconnected voice sound like? What are the telltale signs of the disembodied voice? The primary feature is simply a sound so soft it cannot be heard more than ten feet from the speaker; the sheer lack of volume is the first sign. Lack of volume is often a result of a lack of breath. Breathlessness typically results from upper-chest breathing, which also can be seen by a rise in the shoulders when the person breathes. A tight or tense or constricted sound can be a result of tension in the neck and shoulders, a tension that can be seen when the muscles and tendons in the neck are bulging or the shoulders are hunched or raised up toward the ears. Another manifestation of the disembodied voice is a pitch range that is artificially high or artificially low. Some women keep their pitch range high as a way not to exert authority, as Sarah testified in chapter 2. Some women speak at the bottom of their pitch range, with no breath support, in response to criticism that their voices are too high or unpleasant. The glottal fry Christine talked about is evident in such women. The disembodied voice lacks energy and therefore often lacks clarity. A woman might be able to produce enough sound to be heard, but vocal clarity relies on giving energy to the consonants. If that energy is missing, the sound may be heard, but it will be muddled. The disembodied voice might also manifest in the combination of glottal fry and a persistent upward inflection at the end of declarative sentences, a style of speaking apparently made popular by the Kardashians.[1] The disembodied voice, the voice of the talking head, is rarely an effective voice. Now we will explore how a disconnect from the body can happen.

47

The War on Women's Bodies

In order to understand women's struggle to speak, we need to explore the connection between the messages females receive about their bodies from an early age and their inability to employ their voices as full-body instruments in the service of the proclamation of the gospel. These messages amount to a war on women's bodies. One such message is the unrealistic standard that encourages women to reconcile the shape of their bodies with media-driven standards of the good body. Girls receive the message that the good body is thin, often impossibly thin, and that normal fat gain associated with prepubescence and puberty is understood to be a lack of discipline and will power. Other messages say that the body must be shapely yet thin, making even the thin body wrong. Still other messages say that the natural maturation process is socially and even sexually dangerous, especially if it comes earlier for some girls than for their peers. These are not new observations, and there is a tremendous amount of literature from several disciplines that points to the lifelong feelings of shame, humiliation, and even fear that many women feel at having the sexually dangerous body, the socially unacceptable body, or even the merely non-perfect body. In any case, the character of the girl, who she is, is defined in relation to her body, not her mind or her soul.

So why do women disconnect from their bodies? Because it is precisely women's bodies that make women wrong. A woman's quest for personhood is defined as a quest for the right body, however that right body is defined. The war on women's bodies is fought in many arenas. For the purposes of this book, I will focus on three. The first is the issue of weight, body shape, and body size. This section will receive the most attention because in my experience as a teacher, it is the near-universal experience of women. Of course, I think all my women are beautiful and perfect, but they don't. Even a woman with the culturally approved good body is not likely to believe her body is acceptable. The second reason I will discuss for disconnecting from the body is the issue of traditional gender norms, that is, what is socially expected of girls and women that leads to the loss of Voice, of her right to express herself. This loss of Voice, her right to express herself, her perspectives, what she understands as the truth of her own experience, leads to the loss of the ability to use her physical voice. The third reason I will discuss is the issue of physical and sexual abuse, which leads a woman to disconnect from her body in order to disconnect from her trauma. The war on women's bodies in the case of abuse is not about the actual incident of abuse alone, but also the ways a "boys will be boys" attitude is accepted, especially on college campuses, the silencing of children who know their abusers, and the often brutal treatment in the courtroom of women whose abusers are brought to trial in the legal system.

Body Talk

One would have to be living in total isolation from popular culture not to know that women of all ages and all shapes and sizes are engaged in an all-encompassing wrestling match with their bodies. From a very early age girls become aware that certain shapes and sizes are approved in our culture, and other shapes and sizes receive hearty disapproval. Despite the fact that obesity rates among preschoolers is apparently in slight decline, childhood and adolescent obesity are still highly problematic, with approximately 17 percent of America's youth considered obese.[2] Approximately one in six children is considered obese, yet buying clothes for even the most average and moderately shaped girls' bodies can be an exercise in utter frustration and despair for both parent and child. When one pair of jeans after another is cut too long in the leg and too tight all over, girls receive the clear message that their bodies are simply not long, thin, or lean enough.

The problem does not abate in adolescence or adulthood, and it is much more insidious than a simple Barbie-doll complex, though at the writing of this chapter, Mattel announced a new line of Barbie dolls. The new line includes three new shapes: curvy, tall, and petite; seven skin tones; twenty-two eye colors; and twenty-four hairstyles.[3] The new Barbie made the cover of the February 8, 2016 issue of *Time Magazine*, on which there is an image of a more full-figured Barbie and the question, "'Now Can We Stop Talking about My Body?' What Barbie's New Shape Says about American Beauty." My guess is that the answer to the question "Now can we stop talking about my body?" is no. No, we can't. We cannot stop talking about the shape of Barbie's body. Barbie is a stand-in for all of us. It will be generations before we stop talking about Barbie's body, if we ever do.

The Barbie ideal demonstrates another way girls' and women's bodies are made wrong. Barbie's traditionally impossible shape of buxom breast accentuated by narrow waist is also an unreachable goal for the naturally lean, what some call "skinny," female who wishes she had a more curvy shape. The girl who is slower to develop than her friends, who remains flat-chested when everyone else is wearing a bra, the girl for whom the skinny jeans are too baggy or who has not started menstruating, the adolescent who has to stuff the breast section of the prom dress to make it fit feels as wrong in her body as the girl who has been made to feel overweight or fat.

There are many ways our culture makes women's bodies wrong. Margo Maine, a psychologist who deals with eating disorders through her private practice, shows how wide-reaching is the economic system that would keep women in their places by waging war on their bodies. Maine takes her readers on a methodical journey analyzing advertising campaigns, the ubiquity of magazines promoting a certain body image, the fashion industry, the diet and weight loss industry, modeling and beauty pageants, plastic surgery, the scourge of violence against women, Barbie, the influence of sports and schools, women's healthcare based on studies about men, and more. Any one or two or three of these cultural arenas are familiar to us, and we are accustomed to dealing with them on a personal level. Taken together, it is overwhelming how many dimensions of women's lives are under scrutiny—or attack. Maine makes the case that when it comes to women's bodies, we are talking about war.[4]

In a 1994 study, Mimi Nichter and Nancy Vukovic introduced the phrase "fat talk" to describe the pervasive conversation surrounding weight and body image among girls, teenagers, and young women.[5] Since then a tremendous amount of literature has grown up around the study of fat talk, and in 2000, Mimi Nichter published the book *Fat*

Talk.[6] Fat talk is everything from comments about what one should and should not eat to mentions of dieting, remarks about feeling fat, comparisons of one's body size to that of others and every revealing remark about one's dissatisfaction with one's body, whether one's body is actually thin or fat. Fat talk is a way of disclosing vulnerability while also protecting the self from potential criticism. If I say I am fat before another has the opportunity to tell me I am fat, I let others know how I feel (I am vulnerable), but I ward off the hurtfulness of hearing it from another. If I am skinny, I say I am fat because I want to belong, because the dominant focus of conversation is on being too fat. There is social risk associated with being skinny as well, as the girls who truly do carry more weight may come to resent the thinner girl who engages in fat talk simply to be part of the crowd. For this reason, and because my experience with women's discontent with their bodies includes those who believe they are too lean as well as those who believe they are too fat, I prefer to use the phrase *body talk.* No matter the size of the body involved, body talk is pervasive, and it carries social risk. This is yet one more relational dimension that girls and women have to negotiate.

Body talk, however, is really only a symptom of a deeper problem. Maine's case is that the problem goes deeper than women's self-perception, deeper than consumerism, deeper than the complex of relationships with other women. She makes the case that an economic system and media-driven perception of the good body has been waging war against women. And not only waging war, but waging war with a purpose; the purpose is to keep women in their place.[7]

How can women focus on developing their God-given gifts, dreams, and visions, their vocational calls, if they face constant pressure to look a certain way in terms of size and beauty? The best way to keep women in their place is to instill in them, and to perpetuate, feelings of insecurity about their value as human beings based on appearance. We will see later in this chapter that this war is waged in the arena of gender norms and around the prevalence of physical and sexual abuse as well. This war is waged in public, out in the open, in mainstream media, consumer-oriented big business, the job market, and all social media platforms. The war is waged based on what

Maine considers to be the one remaining politically correct form of prejudice, which she names "weightism."[8]

Weightism is a form of widely accepted prejudice that has resulted in discrimination in the job market, with studies showing close connections between size and hiring and firing.[9] Weightism manifests itself in value systems, with one study finding that more than half of the females surveyed between ages eighteen and twenty-five would "prefer to be run over by a truck than to be fat."[10] Maine cites a study by genetic researchers that "found that 11 percent of parents would abort a fetus that was genetically coded to be overweight."[11] I read these reports with some skepticism. If a truck was barreling down on a young woman and she was faced with making an instantaneous decision to live and be fat or to die, I have to think most young women would choose to live and be fat. But the impulse to respond to the question with such dread of being fat is what we are talking about.

Women do not come to fat talk by themselves; body talk is not encoded in their DNA. Women aren't born into fear and smallness or a desire to take up less space in the world. A woman's genetic makeup does not determine that she be weak, submissive, quiet, cute, or sweet. And the issue is not new. A quick survey of one hundred years of the enviable body size and shape will show how the cultural idea of the good body has changed every twenty years or so, and therefore how elusive is achieving the goal of the culturally approved good body.

In *The Body Project: An Intimate History of American Girls*, Joan Jacobs Brumberg gives a pictorial history of advertisements dating back to the nineteenth century that promote the right body size and dimensions, and products that will help girls and women achieve this body.[12] Some of these advertisements are quaint and humorous to us today, such as the ad from 1903 that promotes Onyx hosiery. As the ankle and even the calf were beginning to be revealed by new fashions, one ad features "The Calf Inspector," with a handsome young man in shirt and tie leaning over a garden wall to smile innocently (or is that a leer?) at a young woman sitting on the grass, reading a book with her full-skirted dress pulled up to expose her calves.[13] Some of the advertisements are more poignant, such as the one for "Chubbettes," which crows, "How happy can a chubby girl be? … As happy as one whose extra young pounds have been delightfully transformed by the designing magic of Chubbettes fashion to make girls 6 to 16 look slimmer."[14] Six to sixteen! Make your six year old look slimmer. What is painfully obvious is that even a six-year-old chubby girl is an unhappy girl unless her chub can be hidden by Chubbettes.

In a *Huffington Post* article of March 2012, we find images of advertisements from the late nineteenth and early twentieth centuries.[15] Soaps are promoted to wash away fat (not so subliminal is the implication that fat is dirty); women are advised to stay slim by reaching for a cigarette rather than a sweet; and the tapeworm diet is introduced so that women can eat, *eat*, EAT and not get fat! Ingesting sanitized tapeworms that will eat away what one no longer needs to resist eating seems preposterous, but the market for preposterous diet schemes is no less vigorous today.

While the intense focus on body shape and size is not new, the correct body shape and size has not been constant over history. In the twentieth century alone, perception of the enviable body shape and size has varied considerably. At the beginning of the twentieth century, the corset-controlled "Victorian hourglass" figure with artificially minimized waist, a buxom bosom, and protruding hips was still the rage. But by 1920, the "flapper" figure was the envy of most girls and young women. Instead of wearing mountains of hair piled on the head as her crown of glory, adolescents and young women began cutting their hair into a "bob," and the corseted figure gave way to the long, slender, flat-chested fashion of the flapper. Young women could easily cut their hair, but often it took serious dieting to reduce from a normal weight to one that had no discernible female shape.[16]

By the end of World War II, larger breasts were back in style, inspired by more full-figured movie stars such as Jayne Mansfield, Jane Russell, and Marilyn Monroe.[17] While this may have eased a bit the need for even the already slender figure to reduce weight, it began the big business of controlling shape with the advent of commercially made brassieres. Mothers took their girls to be fitted with training bras for their new "buds" (the premenstrual swelling of the breasts).

Why did these tiny buds need to be trained? So that they did not sag as they grew. As a young woman's breasts grew larger, she was told that she needed new and often specialized bras to support her breasts so that the subcutaneous musculature structure and outer skin did not stretch to a dangerous extent. Such stretching could threaten her overall health and future ability to nurse children, as the advertising reasoning went, and, of course, the dreaded sagging bosom was to be avoided at all costs.[18] The human race managed to survive for tens upon tens of thousands of years on mothers' milk without sophisticated brassieres to shape and protect women's breasts, but the perceived need to look the right way combined with big business interests and advertising dollars is a powerful force.

The women of the 1960s woke up to this war on their bodies and on their proper place in the world and burned their bras in protest. But as the no-bra hippie look faded, the need to control the body re-emerged. The woman's body in the late 1970s and 1980s was measured by the potential outcomes of the fitness craze. Jane Fonda workouts were all the rage, and training videos such as *Buns of Steel* followed by *Abs of Steel* promised to firm up the most problematic body parts. Slender but still shapely was the ideal, leading to the end of the twentieth century and up to today where not only is slender and shapely desirable, but lean and muscular is envied. Now women want to be lean but shapely, feminine but hard, well-muscled but avoiding thunder thighs and bulking up. In fact, it is difficult for women to bulk up, especially if a woman eats so little that only well-defined muscles show.

This is only a brief and generalized overview of trends of the twentieth century. It primarily addresses the emphases reflected in broadly defined middle-class white America, the target of the biggest share of advertising dollars spent in the twentieth century in America. But it indicates the way in which women's body parts have been scrutinized, valued and evaluated, objectified, and targeted by fashion industries, and how all of this has contributed to the nearly unavoidable self-consciousness of nearly all girls, adolescents, and young women, no matter the shape of their bodies. It is no wonder that body talk pervades our conversation.

The type of body talk prevalent today is not just off-handed comments. When a girl says, "I'm so fat," she is not just stating a verifiable fact. In fact, she may be of a normal, healthy, even enviable weight. She might even be "skinny." But she is probably also insecure about her body. Even at a normal, healthy, and enviable weight, she does not see herself that way; or if she is thin, she worries she will not be able to stay that way; or if she is too thin, she may wish she had more shape, more mass and physical power. Body talk of any kind is a way to elicit feedback from friends. When a girl says, "I'm so fat," what she hopes to hear is, "Oh, no you're not!" There is a dance surrounding such conversation that varies depending on the circumstances and upon the age of the girls, young women, and even older women. Sometimes "I'm so fat" is a prelude to eating something everyone knows is fattening or not good for you. By saying, "I'm so fat" before eating it, the girl is telling everyone around her that she knows what she is doing, she knows she is taking a risk, but she is choosing the danger.[19] So sensitive are women to others' perception of them that many females, no matter their age or size, will pick up an irresistible treat only after saying, "I know I shouldn't be eating this, but..." The message is, "I know this is fattening; I know it can lead to weight gain; but I'm going to eat it anyway. Don't say anything to me about it."

As we can see, body talk and perceptions regarding the correctly shaped female body are not at all new. What is new in the last twenty years is the impact of media and the weight loss industry in fueling perception, talk, and action with regard to weight and size. According to a May 2015 *Fortune* magazine article, the diet and weight loss business was a $60 to $64 billion industry in 2014.[20] This is up from a $34 billion industry in 2000.[21] The $60 to 64 billion figure represents a slight loss from the previous year. At $64 billion, the weight loss industry lost a bit of ground due to a growing interest in eating healthy over using weight loss products such as convenience foods and prepared meals. Health club memberships, medical weight loss programs, and bariatric surgeries, however, are on the rise.[22] One might take some solace in the possibility that our culture is looking more seriously at overall health than at diet, per se, but even the effort toward overall health is focused in the media on the right body.

One dimension of advertising is simply that it plays on the desperation of those who want and/or need to lose weight—for whatever reason. But more subtle and even more insidious is the pervasive message that the slimmer/leaner/thinner body achievable with diet products, gimmicks, and engineered snacks is the right body, the good body. Not only do these products tend not to work as advertised, but the constant assault of their message actually sets the body-image bar higher. Even if the product does not work, and even if we can detect that before and after pictures have been posed and photo-shopped for optimal effect, we still cannot avoid the message and the desire that our bodies look like that "after picture." Even *false* advertising sets the bar higher for the good and enviable (and often unachievable) body.

Five years after publishing *Body Wars*, Margo Maine and Joe Kelly published *Body Myth*, in which they give a lucid and reasonable account of how and why the body of weight loss ads is so difficult, if not impossible, for most women to attain. The "body myth" says "that our self-worth (and our worth to others) is (and ought to be) based on how we look, what we weigh, and what we eat. We look for life's meaning and the answer to life's challenges in the shape of our bodies."[23] The false reality that the body myth reinforces is that "changing my body equals changing my life."[24]

Some might think they have avoided the body myth or perhaps feel relieved that their daughters are not buying into it. I encourage all who believe this to think about the challenge of choosing an outfit every day, of the concerns for makeup and hair, and the tendency when walking into a room to make a quick assessment of what everyone else is wearing and how they look. And then, of course, we make a quick comparison to ourselves. Body myth.

I see the effect of the body myth and body talk on my students. Many women cannot use their voice, their full-body instrument, in service to preaching the gospel without establishing or reestablishing a loving connection between their bodies and who they know or believe themselves to be. Even to say "establish" or "reestablish" a connection expresses the extent of our disconnect from our bodies by suggesting that there is any other way to be who we are besides being in our bodies. We cannot be who we are by being outside of our bodies critiquing them. We cannot be who we are by denying our connection with our bodies. Our challenge is to be our bodies, which is to be who we really are, as God created us to be.

To help my students be in their bodies in service of vocal production, I have found it helpful to encourage them to listen to their bodies as part of their internal Voice. Identifying one's own internal Voice, one's point of view or perspective, with the body itself is a step toward owning both body and voice. Another way to say this is, we cannot fully own our internal Voice if we do not fully own our bodies. Listening to the body can help to drown out other voices from the culture that become internalized and can help ground women in their full-body instrument. This is one key to engaging their physical speaking voice.

Listening to and owning our own internal Voice can be a challenge in and of itself. Maine and Kelly describe one aspect of the internalized Voice of the culture when they discuss the experience of those suffering from eating disorders. Maine and Kelly say that those afflicted with eating disorders listen to the "Voice" of the disorder, something inside their heads that tells lies about their bodies and their lives.[25] The "Voice" tells them they are worthless, ugly, and unlovable, that the unreasonably low number on the scale is a lie, that food is inherently bad, and that eating at all indicates a lack of control. This "Voice" is not actually the person's internal Voice, nor is it the Voice of the gospel. It is the Voice of the illness, the eating disorder. The Voice of the illness, the eating disorder, is a lie; it is telling the woman a lie; it is a liar. This woman needs to discover her own internal Voice, the truth of her own experience that is coherent with who she really is and the value of her own body. Sometimes it is difficult to discern our own internal Voice when there are other strong Voices in our heads.

There may not be a large percentage of women who suffer from eating disorders, but a much larger percentage of women suffer disconnection from their bodies in the form of disordered eating. Disordered eating is a struggle with food that falls short of clinical anorexia nervosa or bulimia, but that still has elements of obsessiveness and distraction, such as continual dieting, yo-yo dieting, and any obsessive eating that breaks the connection between food and the body's messages about good nutritional health.[26] Women of all shapes and sizes struggle with disordered eating, including women who have what might be considered the perfect body. Listening to the "Voice" of disordered eating keeps women in their place, depresses their mood, and puts a damper on their goals and ambitions. By silencing the true needs of the body, disordered eating silences the woman it affects. As a constant preoccupation, disordered eating saps the energy we need to be who we are and who we are called to be, and can make using the physical voice difficult at best.

I have found in my work with women that learning to listen to our bodies is a path to return to the way God created us to be. It is turning away from consumerism's rules about calories and good and bad foods. It is turning toward the natural mechanisms by which our bodies tell us what they need to thrive and serve God. Listening to our bodies is a way to be at one with ourselves, to have the integrity and command of the self that is needed to authentically and authoritatively preach the Word.[27]

Being at one with the body also means listening for and accepting the body's unique needs. Some of our bodies are differently abled, or not as able as they used to be. I am in need of bilateral knee replacement. This means I cannot wear heels, and I am not able to stand in one place for a long time. By the time I have finished preaching a sermon, even all the movement in the pulpit or around a stage does not spare me from the stiffness caused by standing. I can far more easily walk for an hour than stand in one place for twenty minutes. We all have to learn to live with our different abilities and still nurture the best in and from our bodies. I have worked with students who use a wheelchair. They may never feel the full-body base of support from their grounded feet. But we can adapt so that their bodies are as available to them as possible. When these students fully inhabit bodies that the culture may denigrate or underestimate, their witness to the gospel is powerful and authentic.

The concept of listening to the body is not a purely psychological approach to the embrace of our bodies for the use of our voices, nor is it simply self-discovery and emotional healing. There is no good news of Jesus Christ apart from the incarnation, from the indwelling of God in human form. We are horrified at the wounds suffered by Jesus in his trial and crucifixion precisely because we honor his body as fully human and his pain as fully human suffering. Jesus really did suffer because he really did live in a human body. We know God because we know Jesus in a human form.

Women today have an enormous challenge to accept and love their bodies the way they are. One aspect of the gospel claim is that the culture does not have the authority or the right to set the standard for what the good body, the good person, is. If we want to speak with a full-body instrument, we need to inhabit the full-body instrument, inhabit and claim our bodies for the God-given gifts they are.

Gender Norms and Loss of Voice

We turn now to a second reason women are disconnected from their bodies and have so much trouble using their voices. This has to do with either the loss of the ability to express one's opinion or perception of a matter, or having never had the ability or right to express oneself in the first place. In other words, when a girl or young woman has been denied permission to speak her mind, it is predictable that she will have trouble speaking at all. Why are women denied permission to speak? Many women have internalized gender norms that render them mute.

In my role as a preaching and speech professor, countless times a woman has come to me saying that she had a particular view or interpretation of a biblical text, but when she went to the commentaries she did not find her view expressed there. She determined that she must be wrong about the text and proceeded to build her sermon based on what she read in a commentary. My first question is always, *Did you find a refutation of your interpretation in the commentaries?* That is, *Did you find your interpretation named and then an argument for why it is not legitimate or appropriate?* The answer is usually no. Usually nothing is said at all about her interpretation.

If nothing is said at all about the preacher's interpretation of the text, and she has done her homework with her conversation partners, then she may have some level of confidence that she has come up with a new thought, a new direction, a new way of hearing the text on behalf of her congregation. If nothing has been said by the special-ists to refute her hearing of the text, specialists such as the biblical scholars, theologians, and historians (whom I like to call conversa-tion partners), then she may proceed with the next steps of her ser-mon. There are some basic ways that the new thought can be tested. Does it cohere with the central gospel message of Jesus Christ? Does it cohere with what she knows about the view or perspective of the book in which the passage is found? Does it cohere with the ways in which Scripture testifies to God's saving work in the world? If the answer to any of these questions is "no," then perhaps the preacher has wandered too far afield. But if the answer is "yes," then she may well have a new insight on how Scripture comes to bear on the lives of her people.

The way preachers tend to bow to the authority of professional biblical scholars speaks not only to a particular tradition of biblical interpretation, but also to the conditioning of women to seek per-mission to say what they have to say. These kinds of gender norms profoundly affect women's ability to speak. Since the vast majority of commentaries written up to now are authored by Western white men, this amounts to asking Western white men what it is okay to say. It is not a matter of challenging the historic faith; rather, it is a matter of realizing that there are new ways biblical texts can be brought to bear upon contemporary hearers and situations. Women hear things in biblical texts that haven't been heard before and make connections that haven't been made before because their Voices, their experience in and of the world, have not been broadly heard and often not welcome before. I have referred above to what a woman understands as the truth of her own experience. I do not confuse this with the Truth of the gospel, the good news of Jesus Christ who is born, crucified, and risen for us. I speak of what a woman under-stands as the truth of her own experience as a way to express a wom-an's right and need to say how she views the world, to interpret the world from the unique perspective of a woman whose experience in the world is profoundly different from a man's. Sometimes this manifests itself as intuition, a gut feeling, as when a woman senses danger in a social situation or perceives that a patronizing gesture is being masked as graciousness. When our Voices, our truth, are not welcome, then our physical speaking voices become compromised or silenced altogether. Women have not been preaching all that long to all that many people in a media-driven culture where their words might be broadcast beyond their given locale. It will take time for the publications of women scholars to be so prevalent that new hearings might come forth in abundance. Until this abundance of women's truth, women's experience in the world (Voice) is spoken by women's voices, the church suffers loss.

The loss of a woman's Voice tends to lead to the loss of the woman's voice. If a woman cannot reconcile having something to say with having a female body, which will she most likely surrender? She can't escape the female body, so she will either not speak, or she will express the conflict physically in her body while speaking. A woman who has lost permission to speak her mind, or has never had permission in the first place, is unlikely to feel free to use her physical voice in an unrestrained way. Time and again I have seen women who could barely bring themselves to speak above a whisper in class, and then I am stunned to hear them strongly singing solos, even belting solos, in chapel worship. Like Chatty Cathy, they have not received permission to speak their minds, and therefore they find themselves unable to claim the right to speak their minds. They find themselves unable to speak.

In a truly momentous study of girls and women and the developmental turning points in their lives, Lyn Mikel Brown and Carol Gilligan (author of *In a Different Voice*) uncover the quandary girls find themselves in when they reach preadolescence.[28] *Meeting at the Crossroads* recounts a longitudinal four-year study at an all-girls' school. The stability of the student body gave the researchers the opportunity to interview the girls several times as they approached puberty and entered adolescence. One reason for studying the development of young girls at an all-girls' school was to remove as much as possible the variable of the potential silencing effects of coeducation, the need for girls to behave in different or certain ways when boys are present. Before beginning any interviews, the researchers spent a lot of time visiting the school, getting to know the girls, introducing the girls to their study, and fielding questions from the girls about their study.

One of the immediate learnings of the research team in the first year was that they themselves became authority figures that the girls found threatening in the uneven power relationship of adult over girl and researcher over subject. The researchers found that their own compassionate, gentle, sensitive presence and highly evolved interview skills inserted into the girls' lives persons toward whom the girls were suspicious and found potentially threatening. The research team had thought that they would be "safe" in the girls' eyes, and that their time-honored and honed interview techniques would be effective. Nevertheless, when they began their interviews, they noticed that the girls immediately treated the interviews as threatening tests. A well-developed underground communication system spread the word about what questions were being asked, and the girls began to plan their answers in preparation for the test. The team came to discover that their presence changed the conditions of the study they intended in unexpected ways.

At the heart of the problem was the way the methodology objectified the girls, despite the researchers' awareness of that danger and their attempts in their original design to preclude such objectification. The researchers were focused on "Voice" (my uppercase V); they wanted to understand girls' experiences and the experience of developing from little girls into adolescents. The researchers asked four basic questions around girlhood experiences that centered on Voice: "(1) Who is speaking? (2) In what body? (3) Telling what story about relationship—from whose perspective or from what vantage point? (4) In what societal and cultural frameworks?"[29] What they came to discover was that to ask the girls "who is speaking?" and "in what body?" was not to ask them "who is listening?" and "in what relationship?" Even though the researchers were personally involved in coming to know the girls and in interviewing them, their study design had not taken into account who they were as listeners and what relationship they had with the girls. The researchers concluded that these dimensions of their methodology had a deeply implicit male understanding of Voice and body and a story of development that was more about separation than relationship.[30]

Perhaps most profound was their realization that by "staying with their methodology, they were in danger of losing the girls."[31] The researchers revised their methodology, forgoing the neatness of certain kinds of assessment and coding answers to take into account the questions the girls brought to the table and how the growing relationships they had with the girls influenced the work. In *Meeting at the Crossroads*, Brown and Gilligan report their findings through the paradigmatic stories of nine girls.

The most common theme found throughout their interviews was that the girls adapted to the need to be nice as they grew from year to year and did not speak openly what they thought or felt. The need to take care of the feelings of another tended to override the concern for their own feelings. In fact, the researchers titled one of the girl's stories, "The Tyranny of Nice and Kind."[32] The girls learned the value of "'calm' and 'quiet' behavior," but words like "friend," "love," and "relationship" began to lose their meaning when they had to cover strong feelings with calm and quiet behavior.[33]

Another common theme in the girls' stories is how they came to not know what they know.[34] As strong feelings, thoughts, or opinions were covered over with nice and kind, calm and quiet, the girls began to lose touch with what they know and what they think (or, as I have alluded above, their "truth"). As the girls approached age thirteen or so, the phrases "I don't know" and "It doesn't matter" increasingly crept into their stories and responses to questions. Listening carefully, the interviewers were confident that the girls did know something and that it mattered more than they were willing to say. But that was just the problem: the willingness to say was being subdued or lost.

One girl, whom they name Anna, spoke of feeling crazy as she began to wonder what was true and what was not true about what other girls were saying. The girls knew that they were not speaking their own truth within this complex web of relationships that were covered with a veneer of nice, and for Anna this led to wondering if anything another says is really how the other feels. What is the other's truth?[35] One can sense a sort of geometric progression of confusion about what anyone thinks or knows as everyone is playing the game of nice and kind, calm and quiet. Add to that the manipulative behavior that will inevitably come when some seek to communicate what they really think while being nice and kind, or to get what they really want while saying it doesn't matter, and the result is girls thinking they are insane.[36]

Mary Pipher makes a similar observation in her book *Reviving Ophelia: Saving the Selves of Adolescent Girls*.[37] Through her counseling practice and teaching at a small liberal arts college, Pipher sees the ways in which girls change as they enter their adolescent years. The confidence and competence of Erikson's fourth psychosocial stage of development that is in full expression by age twelve becomes one in which the personality of girls seems to disappear.[38] Pipher recounts the story of one girl after another who, until around age thirteen, was bright, inquisitive, resilient, and confident, only to disappear into silence, apparent disinterest in the world around her, and an unwillingness to take risks.[39] Obviously this experience does not describe that of all girls. But Pipher notes, "Adolescent girls experience a conflict between their autonomous selves and their need to be feminine, between their status as human beings and their vocation as females." Then Pipher quotes Simone de Beauvoir, "Girls stop being and start seeming."[40] The vocation of being female is a construct of society. For girls and women who actually have a sense of who they really are, or remember a time when they did, the pressure to reconcile what is expected of them as females and who they believe themselves called to be is extreme.[41]

I see the conflict in the bodies and voices of the women I teach, the conflict between what is expected of women, which is the tyranny of nice and kind, and the call to ministry. The conflict between being female but feeling a powerful sense of call and a fire in the belly for the gospel is reflected in a constrained body posture and restrained vocal production that suggests a woman wants to be agreeable, that she does not want to offend. Sometimes the head is cocked to one side, a demure posture. The tyranny of nice and kind is reflected in vocal tone that is sweet and often high in pitch, and in the upward inflection at the end of declarative statements known as upspeak, or uptalk, as noted earlier in this chapter.[42] A constant laugh or chuckle when one would expect a woman to say something with conviction is an implicit asking of permission to speak. The change to authentic vocal expression happens when a woman is able to both be herself—strong, grounded, authoritative—and also be in relationship with her hearers. I consciously seek to create a classroom and work-shop setting where there is as little conflict as possible between being oneself and being in relationship, where truth can be spoken into a loving space, where a passage about sad events can be read with a sad expression and a passage about violence can be read with an angry expression, where the woman can bring her full-body experience to the text.

Abuse

"You don't know me, but you've been inside me, and that's why we're here today."[43]

So began her victim statement at the sentencing hearing. Addressing her comments directly to the twenty-year-old Stanford University swimmer[44] convicted of raping her, this courageous woman, a Stanford University graduate herself, told her abuser, the court, and the world what a devastating effect his violence against her had on her life. "You don't know me, but you've been inside me ..." After telling the court about her experience at the hospital, the collection of evidence, her slow realization that she had been violated, and the effect of seeing the words "rape victim" on papers she was asked to sign, she said she was finally allowed to take a shower.

> After a few hours of this, they let me shower. I stood there examining my body beneath the stream of water and decided, I don't want my body anymore. I was terrified of it, I didn't know what had been in it, if it had been contaminated, who

had touched it. I wanted to take off my body like a jacket and leave it at the hospital with everything else.[45]

I decided, I don't want my body anymore.... I wanted to take off my body like a jacket and leave it at the hospital with everything else. These words are a profound and powerful expression of this woman's Voice, her truth that affects her voice, her ability to be in her body. It would not change the truth of her experience to tell her that she has been medically examined and physically cleansed and decontaminated from anything that had been inside her. That would not be the truth of her experience, even if it was factually accurate.

The experience of having been abused may not be as universal as women's struggles with body size and shape, or the silencing of women's Voices. Nevertheless, girls and women are abused—physically, mentally, emotionally, sexually—and the abuse happens in the context of their being female and having female bodies. I said in the introduction that what I talk about in this book cannot be said of all women, and can be said of some men. I want to reiterate that here with respect to this section on abuse and the effect abuse can have on the silencing of the survivor. Domestic and sexual abuse perpetrated against men is every bit as grievous as that perpetrated against women, and I have seen the effects on some of my male students. I will proceed to talk about women simply because women are the main focus of the book and not out of a lack of concern for men.

Women are abused both physically and sexually at a far greater rate than many may be aware. The National Coalition Against Domestic Violence (NCADV) tracks domestic violence (DV) statistics generally and intimate partner violence (IPV) in particular.[46]

According to a Center for Disease Control (CDC) survey in 2010,

- every nine seconds in the U.S. a woman is assaulted or beaten;
- in the United States, an average of twenty people are physically abused by intimate partners every minute;
- this equates to more than ten million abuse victims annually;
- one in three women and one in four men have been physically abused by an intimate partner.[47]

The National Sexual Violence Resource Center focuses on sexual assault in particular. They report that

- one in five women and one in seventy-one men will be raped at some point in their lives;
- one in four girls and one in six boys will be sexually abused before they turn eighteen years old;
- one in five women and one in sixteen men are sexually assaulted while in college.[48]

These statistics give us an idea of the scale of the problem. We might think that abuse is more prevalent in some communities than others. But we draw that conclusion at our own peril and at the peril of the girls and boys, the women and men we know and care about, the members of our congregations, our friends, our students. These statistics are debated in some circles, but even if only one in six or one in twelve women have been physically abused by an intimate partner, or only one in ten or one in fifteen women have been sexually assaulted, we still have to face the fact that any woman with whom we interact may have experienced abuse. And we have to consider the effect of that abuse on the woman's body and her ability to use her voice.

The Stanford victim said it as eloquently as possible. As a woman who had experienced sexual assault, she no longer wanted her body. She wanted to take it off like a jacket. A woman who has experienced sexual violence may feel her body is no longer her own, that she isn't whole, that she is not herself. A woman who has experienced physical violence may feel her body isn't safe and that she cannot protect it. A woman who has experienced emotional or psychological abuse may feel that her body is simply not worth being saved.

The sense of not being in the body, not owning the body, not feeling safe in the body goes beyond emotions. Neuroscientists tell us that the trauma involved in experiencing abuse actually creates changes in brain chemistry. The memory of the abuse is not like other memories. "Rather, the trauma gets 'stuck' in the wrong part of the brain. In this part of the brain, trauma is misperceived as ongoing rather than part of the past."[49] When a person has experienced a traumatic event, the memories that persist have the effect of making the person relive the experience over and over again. The person gets stuck. This can lead to the condition called in the DSM-5 "post-traumatic stress disorder," an anxiety response to the trauma that makes it seem as if it is happening again in real time.[50]

The post-traumatic stress experienced by the victims of sexual and physical abuse has long been connected to that experienced by combat veterans. The finding that reliving traumatic experiences actually changes brain chemistry over time, and that this is actually a natural and adaptive response, has led many in the military to drop the word "disorder" altogether. In 2011, General Peter Chiarelli, the Army's vice chief of staff, described how the word "disorder" had a chilling effect on the inclination of soldiers to seek treatment. He proposed calling the condition "post-traumatic stress injury."[51] The argument is that the condition is no different than a physical injury sustained in battle, except that it doesn't actually bleed and it cannot be seen. With treatment soldiers can recover from physical injuries, even traumatic limb injuries. They are expected to seek treatment, and no one doubts the need for treatment. Soldiers who suffer from post-traumatic stress are encouraged to seek treatment because the condition can have an extremely negative impact on a soldier's life long after a physical injury might heal. I have been told by friends in the military that the condition is now routinely referred to as simply post-traumatic stress.[52]

Post-traumatic stress is not the only response to physical and sexual abuse, and not everyone suffers post-traumatic stress in the same way or to the same degree. There are other ways survivors' lives are changed that require treatment and healing. Emotional repercussions for the survivor may include feeling as though she is morally bad and probably deserved the abuse or that her body is bad and in need of punishment. Fear of intimacy and difficulty in trusting others, or, alternatively, becoming overly dependent and submissive in relationships are not uncommon dynamics for the survivor.[53] Physical repercussions for the survivor may include self-mutilation such as cutting or burning, sexual dysfunction, and the tendency to dissociate from her body in times of stress. The survivor may have learned that dissociating from her body was an effective survival tactic while being abused and may unconsciously employ the same tactic in a subsequent time of psychological stress and anxiety even though she is not in an abusive situation.[54] Spiritual repercussions may include feeling punished by God, feeling as though God was not there to protect her in the first place, feeling as though she is not good enough to go before God, or developing a distorted image of God.[55]

Many girls and women who experience sexual abuse know their abuser, which leads to still more devastating repercussions. The Rape, Abuse, and Incest National Network (RAINN) reports that 93 percent of juvenile victims know the perpetrator of the abuse, and 75 percent of all rapes are committed by someone known to the victim.[56] In addition to the crisis of trust this causes the victim, the damage to her other relationships, and the likelihood that the abuse may be ongoing, knowing one's abuser inflicts a silence upon the victim that is hard to break. The primary way a parent or grandparent, aunt or uncle, sibling, coach, neighbor, teacher, or pastor can get away with abusing a child is to silence the child upon threat of great harm to her or to her loved ones, or to the abuser if the abuser is a beloved figure. The ostensible purpose of this silencing, this "don't tell," is for the perpetrator to escape punishment, to escape justice. The silencing of the survivor, however, is an extension of the abuse, a denial of justice, a denial of truth. The silencing consists of the message, "Don't tell about the abuse," which becomes the message, "Don't tell the truth." As we have seen above, denying one's own truth makes it hard to say anything at all. The one who has experienced abuse is silenced not only about the abuse, but may well be silenced altogether.

These dynamics are not unknown to us, but they need to be named in the context of our discussion about women's voices. It can be very difficult for a survivor of abuse to claim her body for the purposes of claiming her voice. She may feel that she is not good enough to speak, that her body is not available for her to speak, that her God is not the kind of God about whom she wants to speak.

This is tragic not just for the survivor but for the church. The experience of abuse is actually part of the church's history and of its theology: Jesus suffered sexual humiliation when he was stripped for physical abuse, and he was physically abused by being beaten and whipped, crowned with thorns, and then nailed and hung on a cross to die. A key tenet of the Christian faith is that God became human and lived out a most extreme form of human suffering. If the church does not hear from those among us who have suffered abuse, we cannot have heard a full witness to the gospel. We tend not to want to hear these things from women who have experienced abuse because it does not feel good, it is unpleasant, even scary, and well, we want things to be … nice. But our gospel is not a nice gospel; it is a True gospel.

The church needs to hear the voices of all who are called to preach the gospel, including women who have experienced abuse, but women who have experienced abuse may struggle to speak and to preach using the full-body instrument. The Stanford University victim testified to how one incident of sexual assault made her not want her body. If I ask a survivor of abuse to speak by exercising her full-body instrument from her feet, the base of support, all the way to the top of her head, I am encouraging her to use the voice God gave her, with the body God gave her, and with the personhood God knew before she was even in her mother's womb. That is my desire for her; I want her voice to speak her own self, her own authenticity, to speak from the truth of her experience, and I want her to be able to speak the Truth of the gospel in service to the reconciling ministry of Jesus Christ. I also know, however, that when I am asking her to use that full-body voice, I am asking her to claim her body in a way she may not be able to do, and that she may not want to do. To reconnect to her body may not only feel unsafe, it may be unsafe if it elicits reliving the physical and emotional sensations of the trauma. The survivor may associate being in her body with upsetting and intrusive feelings, thoughts, and sensations. Her disconnect from her own body may be a survival tactic that helped her at the moment of the trauma and that may continue to assert itself in the present as a physiological consequence of extreme stress. This is exactly what I witnessed when working with Sarah.

While I believe more of my students suffer from the cultural war on the size and shape of women's bodies than have suffered physical and sexual abuse, the effect of suffering abuse and the difficulty the survivor of abuse has in learning again to use her body to speak can be long and difficult.

From a pastoral perspective, judgment of a woman's voice can be supplanted by love and support, encouragement, and a fervent desire for fairness and justice. The redeeming and gracious love of God and the acceptance of a faith community can be brought alongside her to accompany her on the journey toward reclaiming her Voice and being able to use her voice. From an educational perspective, I seek to provide a safe context for my students to refocus on their bodies with the goal of using their voices. Such safe spaces and strategies include doing physical breathing exercises on the floor where none of us can actually see the others, doing such exercises and vocal exercises with eyes closed, and creating a context where sharing experiences and even unrestrained laughter and tears are welcome.

Sarah's story in chapter 2 is testimony that for women who have experienced abuse, the full-body instrument might be very difficult to learn to play. Simply blowing harder into the mouthpiece is not the solution. A woman who has experienced abuse and who cannot make a sound that carries to the back of the room will probably not be able to respond to the encouragement to "throw the voice" to the back wall. It does not solve the problem to tell her, "Stand this way and breathe this way." If the body is inaccessible to her, the body she wishes she could take off like a jacket, then the voice is also inaccessible. But standing and breathing in a certain way can be a first step in feeling what the body needs in order to produce sound.

There are, in fact, many paths to reclaiming the body. One process for making the body accessible again will be explored in chapter 5, "Embodied Voice." I use the exercises explained in that chapter to help my students experiment with new ways to connect with their bodies for the purpose of using their speaking voices. Sarah found hula dancing a creative path to reinhabiting her body in a safe way, though she reports in her story that it took her a long time to take even a step. However it is accomplished, fully inhabiting the body is essential to a full-body speaking voice.

Whether my women are preoccupied by the size and shape of their bodies, or have lost their right to speak their own truth, or have experienced the violation of abuse, we work at restoring the body to its proper place as the heart and soul of our voices. I do not pretend to be a nutritionist, family counselor, or therapist. I do know that God created our bodies, that God created our bodies good, and that God loves our bodies and calls us to love our bodies as well. As students and preachers begin to own their stories and their bodies, they begin to learn to bring their authentic selves and what they know to be true about their own experience in the world to the Truth of the gospel as found in Scripture. They learn to sort out what is a cultural message and what is the gospel message. As they do this, they find the solid ground of the gospel message on which to stand and ground their full-bodied voices in service to the proclamation of the Word.

Conclusion

Why do women struggle to speak? The voice is a full-body instrument, but many women are disconnected from their bodies. In this chapter we have explored just three reasons why women might feel disconnected from their bodies. Women struggle to feel good about the size and shape of their bodies and therefore shrink from their bodies rather than inhabiting them. Women are trained to be nice and kind, calm and quiet, which has the effect of disconnecting them from the truth of their own experience. Women who have experienced abuse may disconnect from their bodies as a survival tactic.

At the center of all of these concerns is the reality of being female. Our bodies are at the heart of what it means to be female. The premise for all three of these dynamics is that it is precisely women's bodies that make women wrong. It is precisely the reality of being female that puts women in a bind. It is not the level of their intelligence or education, whether they are good athletes or mathematicians, or poets or nurturers or business people. It is the body itself that leads to the conflicts we have discussed. It is the fact of being female that leads to the conflicts we have discussed.

In the next chapter, we will talk about claiming our bodies and our truth and what it means to body forth in service to the gospel.

CHAPTER 4

Voice Restored

Many have asked me, when I tell them about this book, how I found my voice. How did I claim my voice? How did I learn to use my voice? The women who tell their stories in the first-person narratives in chapter 2 have been especially encouraging that I need to tell my own story. I resisted because I do not have a dramatic "come to my voice" story. Because of my musical training and the nature of my personality, I thought I always had my voice. In reconnecting to my own story, however, I found connective tissue between my sense of self and my identity, my ability to find and express the truth of my experience in the world, and the use of my voice for proclamation of the gospel. In fact, it was for the proclamation of the gospel that I found my voice, and it was in service to the gospel that I was able to embrace my own truth about my life and my body so that I could seek freedom from any hindrance in preaching.

Our voices are deeply connected to who we are, and my story is no different in that regard. When I was growing up, I consciously thought of myself as a composite of my family members. My father was a management consultant, a plant maintenance engineer, or, as we always liked to say, an efficiency expert. There was a best way to do everything, which was the right way. There was economy of effort with commitment to excellent results. There was a right way to wash the car, to shine shoes, to mow the grass, to make a bed, to roll the garden hose, to pull the weeds, and to sweep with a broom. I believed a part of my identity was to know the best way—the *right* way—to do

everything, and to do it well. And since my father was always right—
always right—I thought that when I became an adult, I would always
be right too. I couldn't figure out when and how that would happen,
but I believed it would happen.

Who was I? I was someone who would know or figure out the
best way to do everything, and I would mostly be right all the time.

My oldest brother, who is seven years older than I am, held the
high distinction in my mind of playing in a marching band. I wanted
more than anything to play in a marching band. Music training in my
house started with the piano. While my parents started my brothers
on the piano in third grade, I could not bear to wait that long. I begged
to start sooner, and they finally gave in, starting me on lessons in second grade. I added the violin in fourth grade (my father studied violin
into a professional repertoire before World War II), the string base in
sixth grade, and the saxophone in seventh grade. In a junior high sum-
mer school class, I learned the fundamentals of percussion and most
wind instruments, though the double reeds and the flute pretty much
escaped me. Like many others of my generation, I taught myself to
play the guitar inspired by the group Peter, Paul, and Mary; Johnny
Cash; and Girl Scout camp songs. I was musical like my oldest brother.

Who was I? I was growing to be right about everything, and I
was musical.

My middle brother, who is two years older than I am, was an
athlete. He got to play all the sports. I nearly died of envy when we
dropped him off at a sports camp at Stanford University one year.
He went to the clinics and learned the fundamentals of the major
team sports, and he played high school football. He would go to
these clinics and recreation camps and learn how to throw and hit
and catch and shoot, and then he would come home and teach me so
that he had someone to practice with. I was a water rat, hitting the
pool whenever possible, and when we went to the beach, I would stay
in the water for hours at a time. I took a diving class my sophomore
year of college and began competing, qualifying for nationals my junior year. I played fast-pitch softball straight through college. I was
an athlete like my middle brother.

Who was I? Mostly right, musical, and athletic. That was me.

How about my mother? Since I was a composite of everyone else in my family, what did I have from Mother that completed who I was? This was a conscious thought process; I would sit in the backyard when I was in grade school thinking this through. How was I like my mother? Mother was a gracious, lovely lady. She did things just right. She kept the house immaculately, with the assistance of her children in household chores. I learned from my mother how to set a lovely table, how to use the china and silver, how to wash it all thoroughly by hand, chip nothing, and leave no water spots. I learned how to be a gracious host.

But I was not a lady. I was, in the language of the day, a "tomboy." Being "overweight" for as long as I can remember, I did not fit clothes very well. The size numbers were always too big for my age; even the modest teasing at school made me feel ashamed, along with the little but constant reminders at home not to eat so much. My mother, on the other hand, looked beautiful in whatever she wore.

Eventually I came to realize that I did not really know who my mother was, and she probably did not know either. She was never allowed to be who she was. If my parents were strict, it was nothing compared to my maternal grandmother, whose husband died at the height of the Depression while she had young girls at home. She scraped to get by, and my mother and her sisters pretty much had to get in line and be good. My mother did not have much of a voice in family matters within her marriage, either, at least as far as I could tell. Even though my father traveled for business every week, leaving Sunday and not returning until Friday evening, and my mother was home alone to do the heavy lifting with the children, it seemed it was my father's presence, his standards, his standing orders that ran the house. That is how I interpreted life.

My conclusion was that I did not have my mother in me.

Who was I? Mostly right, musical, athletic, and decidedly blank. It never occurred to me that I was someone all my own, unique, organically new to the world, one of a kind.

Can it be lost on anyone that the only other female in the family was the one person I did not identify with? I began wondering in early adolescence how this composite picture was going to make its way in the world. There were no visible role models for anything but the proverbial teacher, nurse, or secretary options for my future, so I pretty much assumed I would be a teacher, and I would probably teach music.

The big turning point came for me in junior high when I began to push back against the every Sunday routine of Sunday school and worship. Why did I have to keep doing this church business? "The pastor's sermon is too complicated," I complained one morning while walking back to the car after worship. "I don't understand what he is talking about." This was a rare moment of mild rebellion, and the next moment explained why. There was no conversation, no question asking me more about what I thought or how I felt. My father simply snapped back at me, "It's damn well time you learn to understand!"

I was probably about thirteen years old, a time when even the most typical young teenager is wavering between pushback and obedience, rebellion and returning to submission. I wavered only a moment; there was no way I could go up against my father. I thought to myself, "Oh, I guess I'm supposed to understand." And believe it or not, I went back the next week and listened more carefully, seeking to understand. And I got it. I caught it. I heard the gospel. I heard the Scripture; I heard the gospel claim of God's love for the world in the life, death, resurrection, and ministry of Christ. As family life began to deteriorate, leading up to my father leaving the family a couple of years later, as I began to conclude that how life was going in my house was not the way God intended, with all the anger and fear and depression, I heard the message that what God wants for us is to be found in Jesus.

My intellectual assent to the gospel sustained me a bit. In eighth grade a friend gave me the book *Christy* by Catherine Marshall, whose deceased husband was Peter Marshall, the chaplain to the United States Senate in 1946 and 1947. I had seen the movie *A Man Called Peter*, which told the story of the Scottish immigrant who became a Presbyterian minister. He was pastor to the New York Avenue Presbyterian Church in Washington, DC, and then right after World War II was appointed chaplain to the US Senate. In the movie, Richard Todd preaches bits of Peter Marshall's sermons, and they hooked me.

I discovered that Catherine Marshall not only wrote the book *A Man Called Peter* but also published a book of his sermons, *Mr. Jones, Meet the Master*. I had to have both of those books. This was well before the big chain book stores, of course, but there was a bookstore on Burlingame Avenue, if I could just make my way down there. We were not allowed to go downtown on our own. There was a fear of hippies who would try to hook you on drugs, the pizza parlor being the most dangerous place of all where someone might slip an addictive substance into your Coke. Those were dangerous days!

I sneaked downtown on my bike and into the little bookstore and found on the shelf *Mr. Jones, Meet the Master*. Looking back at the incident now, what was the likelihood of finding that book in 1969? The sermons were the very same as those preached in the movie. They were conversational, human, and strong in gospel claim.

What would a sermon sound like coming from *my* mouth? What did my voice sound like when preaching a sermon? Would that make sense? Could that be coherent with who I was? I did not have a sermon to preach, but I had Peter Marshall's sermons. So in another episode of adolescent subterfuge, I sneaked down the three-mile hill on my bike to my junior high school and preached Peter Marshall's sermons across the ball fields to no one but God—and me. Peter Marshall left clues for how he intended his sermons to be preached. He laid out the sermons on the page in a format that directed the eye and ear to phrasing. The paragraphs were short. There was a lot of indentation and parallel construction. Aside from listening to my own pastor, my first learning for preaching for the ear came from preaching those sermons aloud when I was fourteen years old. I still use his formatting devices when I teach preaching and in my own preaching. And with no one around to constrain me, I heard the sound of my own voice speaking the gospel.

I wandered from my faith in high school. When my father left the family in the fall of my sophomore year, making the shocking announcement at the end of moving day from the big family home we had occupied for seven years to a comparatively small three-bedroom apartment, my world went into a tailspin. There were the usual confusions: I had no idea whatsoever this was coming; we didn't know people who divorced; no one in our extended family was divorced; the shame of it all was overwhelming; we had never lived in an apartment; what were we doing there? And then there were the blows to my understanding of who we were as a family, and therefore who I was.

My father was always right. That is who I was becoming, too. But he left my mother; he left my family. How could that be right? He even told us the night he left that he just felt it was the right thing to do under the circumstances. Leaving my mother and the family was right? How could it be right? But it must be right. Dad is always right. I spent most of high school stuck in the dissonance of this conundrum: Dad is always right; but leaving Mom must be wrong; but Dad is always right; and by the way, if Dad is not always right, how am I to become always right? Isn't that who I am?

Lost, scared, demotivated, confused, angry, depressed—these were the emotions consuming those days. I performed horribly in school, but I clung to my music. I had started to get control of my perennial childhood weight problem in junior high, but now I regained the weight I had lost and more. I stopped going to church even though my mother came into my room every Sunday morning that year and asked if I wanted to go with her. No, I didn't want to go to church. The reality was that I was growing out of my clothes; I felt ashamed of my looks, my weight, and my family. I didn't want to get out of bed. I was miserable.

Christmas Eve, however, at 11:00 p.m. was the high and holy hour of the year at my church, a service I could not bring myself to miss. I could still squeeze into a dress and went with my mother. We got there just on time, which means late, and we had to sit in the balcony. I hated that. We never sat in the balcony. As we climbed the stairs to nearly the top row of the balcony, I tripped on a step and fell forward. My clothes were tight; I wasn't used to being in dress shoes. Now I was miserable and humiliated, confident that the eyes of the whole balcony congregation were gazing at me with condescension and pity: the awkward, overweight girl from a broken family. I spent much of the service trying not to cry.

The sermon that night was titled, "Are You Anybody?," a prescient question. Of course I was not anybody. My pastor's opening illustration was a *New Yorker* cartoon depicting a group of pretentious elites at a cocktail party. One person says to another as they stand by a fireplace sipping their martinis, "Are you anybody?" The sermon proceeded to draw the distinction between what our society and culture understands as "somebody" and what it means to have identity in the eyes of God. I heard the gospel that night. The sermon concluded with this: "I pray that in answer to the question, 'Are you anybody,' you will be able to say, 'Yes, I am child of the living God.'"

That Christmas Eve I went into church thinking that if I was anybody, it was a confused composite of incoherent traits inherited from my family. I still spent a couple more years in my "does not compute" state of mind: Dad is always right; but Dad left Mom and that can't be right. It took me quite a while to realize that Dad was not always right, and I never would be either. But I never forgot that sermon, and I clung to the claim, "I am a child of the living God."

Twisting in the conundrum of "Dad is always right; but Dad left Mom and that must be wrong" was the hint to the problem of my identity. I did not know my own truth; I could not connect to the truth of my own experience. I was so busy buying into everyone else's truth, what everyone else told me was true about our lives, that I did not know I had a truth. I did not know I had a right to my own truth. If I had known, I might have claimed the truth that what my father did to my mother and the family was wrong. He figured that out himself, and four years later came back and remarried my mother. And in the years to come, I would figure out that my mother was *smart* (why did I not see that before?), a woman of strong backbone and iron will. To this day I'm not sure if I have ever met anyone of her perseverance and determination. Mostly right, musical, and athletic. And I could only hope one day to have the strength of my mother.

I got into college on the merits of my music, taking with me one truth that dawned on me on my eighteenth birthday: my life was my own. My father was responsible for neither my weight gain, nor my poor grades, nor my moods. I was responsible. I could make something of my life, or I could give up. I decided to make something of it. I learned to study; I switched majors from music to political philosophy and rhetoric. I began to sense again the call that I had felt as a fourteen year old. And I discovered that the Truth of the gospel was the big Truth, the fundamental Truth, the Truth that made sense of all the other truths. For the first time in my life, I was succeeding at my endeavors under my own power and my own motivation, inspired by the notion that I was valued in the eyes of God and that God had a plan for me.

My weight came down; my confidence rose. My pastor used to talk about every thought being brought into the captivity of Christ. I found in my studies a rich foundation for philosophical thinking, examining fundamental assumptions in an effort to get underneath how things appeared to find what truth lies beneath. I had no trouble seeing how all of this was in service to Jesus Christ and his ministry. I was learning to find truth, and I was filling in the spaces of my own truth.

My truth was found in the simple gospel acclamations: I am a child of the living God; I am saved by grace through the Lord Jesus Christ; my life in Christ is sustained by the ever-present Holy Spirit; the Scriptures will guide me by the counsel of the Holy Spirit into life lived in conformity to the will of God. These were my truths. They did not start and end with my father or my family or even with me. They started and ended with the one true living God. I came to believe that God was calling me to preach this good news, that my voice, the physical mechanism that preached Peter Marshall's sermons to the ball fields at my junior high back when I was fourteen, was being called to preach this good news to real people.

The good news had saved me. It had saved me from utter despair and confusion. I had not yet figured out completely who I was in rela-tion to my family or how I would manage my lifelong, errant, subtle, and diminished but ever-present expectation that I would somehow become mostly right someday. I still remember working with a dear friend in ministry to prepare a music program for a senior citizen group. We were going to do our version of "The Battle Hymn of the Republic," and at the piano, I knew exactly how it was supposed to go. I pressed my case for a very slow tempo for the last verse: "In the beauty of the lilies Christ was born across the sea ..." We were not the Mormon Tabernacle Choir. We were just two. I was insistent. My friend asked me with exasperation if I thought I was always right. Well, not always, but musically? Yes, I thought with some bemusement, I usually am! That's my job.

The good work God had begun in me was nowhere close to being finished, nor is it yet. But I knew from whence my help came, and I knew I was being called into the ministry of showing others from whence comes our salvation.

My truth was found in the gospel. The acceptance of my family history was found in the grace of Jesus Christ. The acceptance of my body, which admittedly was easier when I was leaner and succeeding athletically, was found in the knowledge that God knew me before I was formed in my mother's womb and loved me no matter my size and shape.

My truth was also found in my calling to use my voice to make that gospel sing. Long before I read Kathleen Norris's observation that we should be wearing crash helmets in church, so profoundly earthshaking is the good news, I wondered why people did not read Scripture with more energy and passion. I wondered why the preachers I heard in college did not preach with the conviction of my home pastor. There is no other good news like this! There is no other truth like this. I was dedicated to making the Truth of the gospel come alive through speaking and preaching, through using my voice.

When it came to using my voice, the truth became of first importance to me. Speaking the truth became an obsession. If it was crushing that my father left my mother and my family, it was virtually paralyzing that I had no idea it was coming. It felt like my home life was a lie. My security was a lie. That lie was so debilitating and so hurtful when I was a teenager that I began to believe that while truth-telling might hurt, it was less hurtful than lying. One of my mantras became this: less people will be hurt less often and less badly by telling the truth. One consequence of this mantra is that I have become not the most subtle or diplomatic person, and this because I am moved to speak out loud the conviction on any matter I feel in my belly.

How did I find or discover or claim my voice? I found it in the gospel. In the ministry of preaching and teaching and sharing the good news, I found a home for every worthy idea and thought I had ever encountered. I found a place where every single note I had ever played on an instrument could be a sweet, sweet sound in God's ear. I found a place where my body, when employed in coherence with the way God designed it, could speak powerfully the Truth of the gospel. The gospel was a Truth I could speak with full conviction, not worried about whether it meshed with any other person's truth, or some external parental measure of what was right. The simple answer to how I found, discovered, claimed my voice is that I found it in the good news of Jesus Christ. I did not go to seminary to find it. I did not need a preaching professor or even a speech professor to encourage me to use it. When it came to the preaching ministry, my voice was free.

Yet, not entirely.

I thought it was. But I was still bound by the intellectualism of my Reformed tradition. And I am sure I found some safety in living in my head. Already given to strong emotions, I did not feel free to be completely expressive in my preaching. After the years I taught preaching at a Baptist seminary, I used to observe that when Reformed and Presbyterian types err, they tend to err on the side of the intellect—they think more than they feel. And when Baptists and Holy Spirit traditions err, they tend to err on the side of emotions—they feel more than they think. I used to want to express more passion and conviction for the gospel than I felt my tradition allowed. I am confident that deep inside of me was a resistance to the gender normative assumption that men are rational and women are emotional. I associated rationality and intellectualism with legitimacy, and I think I feared strong emotion in preaching, which I feared that in my tradition might be labeled some form of female hysteria.

Looking back, I know I wanted my whole self, my whole body, to be available to me in the use of my voice in preaching the gospel. I used to worry that not feeling free to express the full range of emotion I felt toward the gospel was in effect embarrassment of the gospel. Being immersed in a community full of Baptists and Pentecostals, Assemblies of God, and Free Church people and preachers gave me permission to increase the range of emotion I was able to express in preaching. I had to get outside my tradition in order to find my true self and the full range of my true voice. It was like getting outside my own family to figure out who I really was. It was like leaving home in order to have permission to become who you really are.

My call to help women use their full-body instrument in service to the gospel required that I claim the truth of my own experience, and the Truth of the gospel, with my intellect, my emotions, and my body. In order to fulfill that call, I had to let myself think and express my thoughts, feel and express my feelings, and be in my female body and allow my body to be. In fact, it was critically important for my students, especially my women students, and for my own daughters, that I be fully embodied, a feeling and thinking human being, and that I *not* obsess over my body, or limit my emotional range, or stunt my intellect. I knew that a focus on my body, an out of control self-consciousness, would not enhance my ministry or make the gospel more compelling or make me a better teacher—quite the opposite. I had to become an advocate for one of the first rules in speech communication in ministry: *it's not about you.* It is certainly not about your shape and size. Even though many of the pages in this book appear to be about the speaker, her body, and her voice, all of this discussion is toward the end that we may freely, authentically, and boldly witness to the good news of God in Jesus Christ by the power of the Holy Spirit. It is about the good news of the gospel, which is abundant life and freedom from cultural expectations, freedom from powers that would silence and crush us, freedom from the effects of abuse, and this freedom is not for our sake alone, but freedom that we may be a sign and witness to others, and thereby bring glory to God.

Body Forth

I learned through my life journey that Truth resides in the gospel of Jesus Christ, and that when it comes to speaking the good news of Jesus Christ, there is a need for the gospel to reside fully in our bodies. Truth and the body go together. Every body has a unique experience and perspective, an embodied perspective, to bring to the whole church. Reading Scripture is not merely a mental exercise. Preaching the good news is not only the out-loud literary result of an interpretive process. Engaging in the liturgy of the church, whether in historic forms or the more contemporary leading of a praise song, is more than the role of a traffic controller. The good news comes not only through our minds and the mechanics of our mouths, but through our bodies and our personalities.[1] Every act of worship calls for a surrender of the total integration of the body-mind-personality-soul. I consider this part of what is meant when Paul says, "present your bodies as a living sacrifice, holy and acceptable to God, which is your spiritual worship" (Rom. 12:1). Present your bodies to the service of God. Bring forth your bodies to the service of proclaiming the good news. Bring forth your bodies; bring forth your whole selves to the people of God.

Bring forth your bodies. I ask my students essentially to present their bodies as a living sacrifice, to "body forth" when speaking in and for a public context. Imagine greeting a congregation by not just mouthing the words "Good morning," but with a full-body expression of the good news, stepping forward with arms open in a welcoming way and saying, "Grace to you and peace from God our Father and the Lord Jesus Christ" (Rom. 1:7b; 1 Cor. 1:3; 2 Cor. 1:2; Gal. 1:3; Eph. 1:2; Phil. 1:2; etc.).[2] When I say "body forth," I am referring to an act where the speaker sends the message out to the hearers from the full-body experience of the message and with the use of the full-body instrument. The message comes from the bodily center, which is just below the breastplate, not the mouth or the head.

To body forth is to hold nothing back. It is the most hospitable act I can imagine for the preacher to offer her whole self in offering the Word to her hearers. When the preacher bodies forth the Word in Scripture reading, she doesn't merely say, "Let me remind you what this Scripture passage is about." When the preacher bodies forth the Word in sermon, she does not merely say, "This is a good idea; you should think about it." Rather, she is saying, "This Word has a hold on my life, on my whole self, and it has a hold on your life as well." The Word saves when it comes alive in us. When we allow the Word to come alive in us and are open and vulnerable and willing to allow our whole body to be involved, we invite the Word to come alive in our hearers.

This idea of hospitality in using our voices is not unlike the hospitality we practice in our homes. Under most circumstances when guests come into our homes, we offer a beverage, a comfortable place to sit, perhaps a snack. Especially if our guests have been invited for a beverage or snack or meal, we certainly offer it to them and do not expect them to have to ask for it. And even if we were somehow distracted, and a guest or even surprise visitor did ask for a glass of water, we would not be reluctant to provide it. We call people to worship, and they expect that we will lead them in worship. They have every right and reason to expect that we will lead them. I encourage my students to extend themselves, to extend their voices to the congregation in the same way they would extend hospitality in their homes. We take our voices to the people. We extend our voices all the way out to all the people. If as a listener I feel as though I need to crawl up to the pulpit or lectern or stage to hear the preacher or worship leader, I do not feel as though my participation is welcome or my listening is expected.

The authenticity or truthfulness with which the preacher extends herself to her hearers and bodies forth the Word also matches the Truth of the gospel. Alla Bozarth-Campbell uses the phrase "body forth" when she talks about Wallace Bacon's theme of "matching."[3] For Bacon, "matching" is the coming together of the body of a poem or a piece to be given oral interpretation (think Scripture or sermon) and the body of the performer or reader or oral interpreter.[4] Neither reader nor Scripture disappears in this matching; rather, the reader seeks *congruence* between herself and the Scripture reading. "It is perhaps not too much to suggest," says Bacon, "that ideally there is a love relationship between reader and poem."[5] Bacon was a secular theorist in performance studies, but it is not a stretch to see how "perhaps," to use his qualifier, a reader must love herself in order to love the other in the form of a Scripture reading, sermon, or other sacred text. This conforms to what Jesus described as the second part of the "greatest" commandment, to love our neighbor as ourselves. When we love ourselves, we are in congruence with ourselves, with our bodies, enabling us the freedom to speak. This freedom is manifested in posture, breath, vocal tone, and vocal gesture. When we lack self-love, we will find it difficult to be congruent with ourselves and therefore find it difficult to speak in congruence with the gospel.

Bozarth-Campbell reports that Bacon described bodying forth as "reverberation." Reverberation is what happens when a reader so embodies a Scripture that it comes alive inside the reader. There are "repercussions in the life stuff" of the reader when the Scripture is allowed to come alive inside the reader; the reader becomes what the Scripture expresses as the Scripture comes alive inside the reader.[6] I have called this "lending the body" to the text. The Scripture awaits not just our voices in the typical sense of the word, the sound that comes out of our mouths; rather the Scripture awaits our bodies to inhabit in order to come alive. The Word reverberates in the core of our being, the core of our bodies. The Word is to become incarnate in us.

Extending our voices, extending ourselves, extending our personalities is part of what is meant when I say body forth, or lending our bodies to the Word. We give to the Word what it needs to be heard. As I said above, what the Word needs comes from our core, from the center of our bodies, from just below the breastplate. Mechanically that means it comes from the power center of the instrument, the abdominal cavity, which includes our bowels. For the ancient Hebrews this center was the core of life, the core of our being, the center of our humanity. When the psalmist confesses in Psalm 51 that God desires "truth in the inward being; therefore teach me wisdom in my secret heart" (Ps. 51:6), I read beyond the traditional understanding of this confession, that we are born into a state of sinfulness from which we need cleansing. I believe this is true. But I also think that for women who have lost the ability to know the truth of their own experience, their own center, their own authenticity, this is a prayer for restoration. For some women, that which needs to be "purged with hyssop" is the brokenness that prevents them from offering themselves and their voices fully to the service of the gospel.

If the voice is a full-body instrument, and it is, then to give to the hearers a rendering of a Scripture text requires an offering of the reader's body, bodying forth. In the speech communication world, we talk about "performing" the Word. To render a poem, a Scripture passage, or a sermon is to "perform" the piece. "Perform" and "performance" are contended words and the subject of countless books and articles.[7] The word "perform" brings to the minds of many people a theatrical act, something that is fake or not authentic. This is certainly one connotation of the word. The etymology of the word "perform," however, is not specifically theatrical. Our word "perform" is derived from the fourteenth century through the Anglo-French word *performer*, to "'carry into effect, fulfill, discharge,' ... altered (by influence of Old French *forme* 'form') from Old French *parfornir* 'to do, carry out, finish, accomplish,' from *par-* 'completely' ... + *fornir* 'to provide.'"[8] To perform is to carry into effect, to fulfill, to provide, and to accomplish. It is to completely provide. When we read a Scripture passage to our congregations, we are lending our bodies to the Word in order to completely provide and fulfill the intention of the Word. We body forth the Word of God. Not to body forth the Word that reverberates in us is to withhold our own conviction about the Word of God.

Many talk about "finding" their voices in preaching. Finding one's voice for preaching is not done merely by finding a vocal range or range of expression. Finding, discovering, and claiming your own voice is not just about finding yourself in terms of your personality, your hopes, desires, dreams, talents, and loves. Finding, discovering, and claiming your voice has to do first with discovering a love for your body as yourself and claiming your body's worth just the way you are, with claiming God's creation of your body and yourself as good and letting that gospel Truth be louder and more resonant than the voice of cultural expectations, the voice of any other powers, or the experiences of abuse. Finding, discovering, and claiming your own voice has to do with allowing the Word to reside in your body and giving your body over to the speaking of the Word—lending your full-body instrument to the Word in order that it may be fully heard.[9]

The Female Vocal Cord

We have noted throughout the book that at the core of being who we are as women, at the core of being in our bodies, is being female.

Here I actually mean female in the sense of the physiological makeup of the body, which precedes even the notion of what it means to be a woman. The gender assigned at birth that we name "female" is also a construct that is in flux today. We know that the designations female and male are more of a spectrum than strict binary concepts. That is yet one more discussion that is outside the scope of this book. For the purposes of talking about female vocal cords, however, I think we can say that the extent to which a person's physiological makeup is female is the extent to which her full-body instrument is affected by female physiology. This refers in particular to the structural makeup of the vocal cords, the effect of hormones on our physical speaking voice, and the changes that often occur as we age.[10]

The image of vocal cords that is likely to come to mind is a number of small strings, or cords, somewhere in the throat. The word "cords" gives to this image a sense of strength and hardiness, durability. Electrical cords have substance; we use cords to hold things up and bind things together. Our vocal cords, however, are better known as vocal "folds." They are not a set of numerous strings but two thin layers of tissue that vibrate as air passes through them. They are not tough but rather delicate. If the abdominal cavity is the center of the motor of sound production, the vocal folds are where the sound is actually created by their vibration when the air passes through them. The head (actually the whole skull), but primarily the throat, nasal cavities, and mouth, are all resonators. The resonators are where the basic sound produced by air passing through the vocal folds is enhanced and given timbre and shape. When we resonate at the back of the cavity, between our ears, the sound is velvety and sonorous. When we resonate at the front of the cavity and engage the jaw and nose, the sound is sharper. A nasal sound is produced when resonating primarily in the nose. The hard palate, soft palate, tongue, teeth, and lips are the articulators. They give shape to the sound to make speech.

Are female vocal folds different from male vocal folds? Again, we have a spectrum. Female vocal folds are likely to be shorter and thinner. Male vocal folds are likely to be longer and thicker. Just as a shorter and thinner instrument, such as the flute, creates sound at a higher pitch than a longer, thicker instrument, such as a tuba, so the shorter, thinner vocal folds of a female will produce a sound higher in pitch. This is one way in which female vocal folds are different from male vocal folds. For this reason, a very large man may have a surprisingly higher-pitched voice simply because his vocal folds are shorter and thinner than we imagine a large man would have. Again, there is a spectrum. The operatic coloratura soprano, the highest pitch range of human voices, is able to produce clarity in trills and runs that not even a female alto voice can produce, let alone a male voice.[11] Yes, there is a difference between female and male vocal folds.

The fluctuation of female hormones may have an impact not only on a woman's mood, weight, and energy levels, but on her vocal folds and voice as well. Falling levels of estrogen may produce a sound deeper in pitch, a loss of vocal range overall, hoarseness, and vocal fatigue. Fluid retention will make the vocal folds bulkier, leading to some of the same effects. When women are pregnant or nursing, estrogen levels increase, which may result in breathiness, a muffled sound, and, again, vocal fatigue.[12] We read in chapter 2 that Christine noticed her voice changed when she was expecting her period. She was not imagining things.

Vocal health or hygiene can be nurtured by staying well hydrated and avoiding screaming or yelling and excessive throat clearing, which result in the vocal folds banging together rather than delicately vibrating together. Nodules, which are like callouses, form when the vocal folds are subjected to this banging together, resulting in hoarseness, a narrowed and lower pitch range, and inability to control one's breath for phrasing—the air escapes too quickly. Warming up the voice before demanding speaking events and avoiding smoking and heavy drinking (which dehydrates) are also features of good vocal hygiene.[13] As we age, the vocal folds are subject to the same kinds of effects as the rest of the body. A narrowed and lower pitch range will result if the speaker does not train her voice with proper exercise. The reduction in estrogen production will also contribute to a lower pitch range. As muscle tone fades, many speakers find they no longer have the abdominal support they once enjoyed.

But with proper vocal hygiene and exercise, the effects of aging can be somewhat mitigated.

Can women go through life and be effective preachers and speakers without knowing anything about the female vocal folds and how to keep the vocal mechanism healthy? Yes, of course. In order to exercise the full-body instrument, however, it is to our advantage to know a little about how the instrument works and how to care for it.

Conclusion

We have discussed in this chapter the voice restored. It is a journey of integration of the truth of our own experience, the claiming of our body, the willingness to give our body over to the proclamation of the Word, and the nurturing of the vocal mechanism that gives shape to sound and meaning to speech. There is precious freedom in being given permission to be in our bodies, to learn to nourish and nurture our bodies for the purpose of expressing our own truth and the Truth of the gospel, and knowing all along that it is not really about us at all. It is about the self-giving that is made possible by self-love, a giving of ourselves made possible by loving our bodies, a love that is mandated by the gospel message, not prohibited. In the end it is about being free to witness to the redeeming grace of our Lord Jesus Christ, the love of God, and the fellowship of the Holy Spirit.

This leads us to ask, *How can we go about learning to use our full-body instruments?* How can we embody this Word? In the next chapter, we will reflect briefly on the story of our lives through the lens of our voices and conduct exercises to learn how to use our full-body instruments.

CHAPTER 5

Embodied Voice

In the last chapter we discussed the need to discover a love for our own bodies and to claim our body's worth in order to allow the Word of God to fully inhabit our bodies. These are what allow us to body forth. In this chapter we will pursue a strategy for connecting our bodies and our physical voices.

When I begin a workshop with women on the use of their voices, I always begin by asking them to reflect on their own voices, how they would describe their voices, a bit of their experience with their voices. I ask them to reflect on how others have responded to their voices or commented on their voices. I want to know the story of their voices.

Vocal History

I ask the following questions.

1. Give three to five adjectives that describe your literal physical speaking voice.
2. In what ways did you find greatest pleasure employing your voice as a child? Do you still use your voice in that way today? How? Or, why not?
3. In what ways did you find greatest pleasure employing your voice as an adolescent? Do you still use your voice in that way today? How? Or, why not?

4. Has your voice ever been critiqued? In class? By church members? What was said?
5. How did you respond to the critique?
6. What is your favorite speaking context? Where do you most like to speak publicly?
7. What is the most memorable sermon you've ever heard? Who preached it? Do you remember the preaching voice? What was distinctive about it?
8. When and where have you been encouraged to use your voice? Where has been the permission-giving?
9. When and where have you been *discouraged* from using your voice? Where has permission been withdrawn?

Not everyone has an answer to all of these questions. Not all of these questions are pertinent to everyone. Since most of the women who come to my workshops do so because they have issues with their voices, nearly all of them have a story about how she used her voice as a child or adolescent and how the way she uses her voice has changed through her adult years.

I am not a speech pathologist. Nor am I certified in Yoga, Pilates, or voice methods such as Linklater's Freeing the Natural Voice, or the Knight-Thompson Speechwork method.[1] What I have is an eclectic combination of skills, training, experience, and knowledge about the body and how it produces sound, pastoral awareness of women's issues with their bodies, and theological conviction about the gifts women bring to ministry. What follows is an approach to reclaiming the use of our bodies and a deep knowledge of our bodies that we were born with for the purpose of producing sound with our voices for the sake of the gospel ministry.

1. Give three to five adjectives that describe your literal physical speaking voice.

Starting with the questions posed above, I ask women to take stock, right now in the moment, of how they would describe their voices. Sometimes women use adjectives that *they* think describe their voices; sometimes women use words others have used. Some have a combination of words. It is important to note if you have your own words. This is part of knowing your own truth. Stop and think about what those three to five words are. Are they positive? Negative? Are they judgmental? Have you ever stopped to even think about that before? Whose words are they?

2. *In what ways did you find greatest pleasure employing your voice as a child? Do you still use your voice in that way today? How? Or, why not?*

If we can get back to a time before self-consciousness set in, we can often remember ways of using our voices that gave us great pleasure. Some were criticized or even punished for using their voices in the ways that gave them pleasure, such as when their voices were too loud, or they talked too much. This was the case with Gi as we read in chapter 2. As noted in chapter 3, at around nine or ten years old, the tyranny of nice and kind begins to develop in girls. The use of the voice may become distant from the core of our sense of self or sense of our own truth. More often than not, women report that they do not use their voices the same way they did as girls. Someone or something has stolen their joy. I try to help them reclaim that joy.

3. *In what ways did you find greatest pleasure employing your voice as an adolescent? Do you still use your voice in that way today? How? Or, why not?*

The questions about the use of the voice through life's stages give women an opportunity to rethink their journey in terms of their voices. So often we think of our life story in terms of family of origin, racial or ethnic identity, places where we have lived, relationships, education, or work. I ask women to recast their stories through how they used their voices and how people have responded to their voices. Sometimes, as in Christine's case, this serves to disclose a painful chapter or person of influence in her life. By bringing that issue into our awareness in our work together, we have the opportunity to replace a negative, critical Voice with another that affirms her identity and calling. Think through your life story with your voice being the main character in the story. How has it developed? How has it changed? How have people responded to it? How do you feel about your own voice through the various stages of your life?

4. Has your voice ever been critiqued? In class? By church members? What was said?

Many women have already been in contexts where they have received feedback about their voices. Sometimes that feedback was helpful and constructive, especially if they had formal training. Often that feedback was not helpful. One pastor has sought me out for voice work because she is constantly criticized by church members and elders at her first called pastoral position. She preaches regularly. After listening to her recordings and watching her videos, I can hear and see what is bothering her parishioners. But the problem is not as bad as she thinks it is, or is made to think it is, nor is any of the feedback she is receiving helpful. Vague comments about not being able to hear usually mean the speaker cannot be understood. While some speakers literally cannot be heard because they do not produce enough sound with their voices, it is more often the case that vocal clarity is lacking.

One comment frequently heard by women is simply that their voice is unpleasant. This goes straight to what might be a subliminal issue about the voice sounding "nice." Congregations tend to want women preachers to have "nice" voices, which means not offensive in any way, which usually has to do as much with the content of the woman's speech as with vocal quality.

During the 2016 presidential campaign, especially during the primary season, there was a tremendous amount of criticism of Hillary Clinton's voice. The public and media outcry about Hillary Clinton's voice is not only sexist at its core (were Bernie Sanders and Donald Trump a pleasure to listen to?); it is also completely misdirected in terms of vocal analysis. It is sexist not only because the same critical attention was not directed toward the male candidates, but because we have expectations that a woman's voice be, well, pleasant. Read here the tyranny of nice and kind. A woman's voice should make us feel good.

The nature of Hillary Clinton's voice had absolutely nothing to do with her character, her personality, or her qualifications for the job of president of the United States. Rather, the nature of her voice, and how she uses it, had a lot to with its overuse and abuse. I do not know if any of the candidates had vocal coaches, but they should have. The excessive use of the voice that is required of candidates in presidential election politics, especially during the primary season, will invariably lead to vocal distress, if not disease, if the voice is not properly trained and used. A person trained in voice can see that Clinton's neck and throat muscles and tendons were strained, meaning that she was trying to produce the sound from her neck and chest, and not from the abdominal center. A person trained in voice can hear that Hillary Clinton's vocal folds were swollen and likely raw from banging against each other, not only from overuse, but also from pushing from the throat for volume and power.[2] Vocal folds, not cords but folds, are delicate layers of tissue that vibrate as air is passed through them. When we cough, or clear our throats, or yell and scream, the vocal folds are not delicately vibrating but actually banging against each other, causing damage. Damage leads to "nodules," which are like callouses, and nodules compromise vocal quality. The primary symptoms are hoarseness, a narrowing of the pitch range, and a lowering of the pitch range. Sometimes loss of voice ensues. What has been attributed to Hillary Clinton as a "bark" is actually a vocal mechanism that is fairly well damaged, hoarse with a narrow pitch range. The only cure is rest, vocal rest. This is not easily accomplished for presidential candidates, or for preachers.

Often when a woman I am working with has had either professional training or speech work in seminary, what we end up discussing is an issue about which she is already aware. We each usually end up working on one specific issue all of our lives. My main challenge is that I tend to drop to the bottom of my pitch range. My speech teacher in seminary constantly told me to raise my pitch. That is still a lingering issue; I tend to speak toward the bottom of my pitch range.

There is positive, helpful feedback that can teach us what to listen for so that we can self-critique and correct.

As we could see in the stories of Chatty Cathy, Sarah, and Christine in chapter 2, many have knowledge and experience of their voices as girls that changes over time. I encourage women who have been silenced in any way to go back and reclaim the right, the joy, and the knowledge of using their voices that they had before being silenced.

5. *How did you respond to the critique?*

Usually women already know how they have responded, or more likely reacted, to the critiques they have received about their voices. And usually the reaction is to drop in pitch or force a louder sound without adequate understanding of how the instrument works. Forced volume without proper breathing produces a strained sound and is damaging to the vocal folds. Part of the process is to identify not only how we have adjusted the voice to answer the critique but also what effect the criticism has had on the speaker emotionally and psychologically. Physical speaking voices can be retrained. As noted in Christine's story, confidence is harder to restore, and healing the psyche takes time and reassurance.

Another response to critique might be accurately described as reaction. Many women will become more reserved, speak more quietly and less often so as not to offend, take on a little-girl tone, or lose the ability to make eye contact with her hearers. The only thing these reactions accomplish is to sound more "nice and kind, calm and quiet." But then, this might be the result desired by the one who leveled the critique.

6. *What is your favorite speaking context? Where do you most like to speak publicly?*

After thinking so much about the criticism we have received about our voices, it is good to revisit the times and places where the use of our voices gives us joy. Some people don't really enjoy preaching all that much. Perhaps there are other reasons for not enjoying preaching that are manifested in how the voice is used. Many people who do not enjoy preaching simply do not think of themselves as "preachers." They may need a different kind of image for who the preacher is than the image they have been given. If the answer to the question is that the person does not really like speaking in a public context at all, then we can talk about what it means to develop this skill as one means of fulfilling the overall ministry. Sometimes people just need permission to say they don't like speaking in public, and preaching is simply an extension of that distaste.

Developing an image of oneself as a preacher requires a bit more soul-searching. Most of the women I have worked with who did not see themselves as preachers were never given permission to preach, or their image of a "preacher" does not match who they are. When I hear such women preach, it is usually clear to me that they do have a preacher's voice—it is their own voice. When I hear them speaking in their natural, authentic voice, I tell them, "*There* it is; that is a preacher's voice." They have to learn that the voice they have qualifies as a preacher's voice because God has called that voice into service.

7. What is the most memorable sermon you've ever heard? Who preached it? Do you remember the preaching voice? What was distinctive about it?

Some of us carry voices of preachers in our heads. If one or two preachers have been particularly powerful or meaningful in your life, considering the tone and quality of their voices might be a hint into how you use your voice or what you find meaningful. We do not want to sound like someone else; we want to sound like ourselves. Is it possible that a dimension of the power of the sermon or preacher you carry around with you has to do with the authenticity of that preacher's voice? Could it have to do with how connected that preacher's voice was to her or his person? Sometimes when we identify this voice, we discover we are trying to sound like that person. It is not uncommon to want to emulate a mentor. The best way to emulate a mentor, however, is to do it with your own authenticity. If it wasn't caught in seminary, if someone did not say to you in a preaching or speech class that it sounded like you were trying to sound like someone else, or even that you sounded like the "proverbial preacher," such habits may continue long into your ministry.

8. When and where have you been encouraged to use your voice? Where has been the permission-giving?

In chapters 2 and 3 we looked at some of the ways women lose permission to speak and how we come to ask permission to speak. We have seen that asking permission to speak is manifested when a woman tries to minimize her physical posture, seeking to take up as little space as possible. Asking permission is manifested with a voice that is small, perhaps higher in pitch in order to sound nice and kind, and often with the tell-tale upspeak, which is raising the inflection at the end of phrases as if asking a question. Now consider the times, places, and spaces where you have been encouraged to speak. When has your voice been welcome? When have you been given permission? Who offered the encouragement? The answers to these questions may still not be entirely affirming. It might be that permission was given for the voice to be used in gender normative ways that did not offend anyone. Nevertheless, it is important to look back and see where and how and by whom we have been encouraged to speak.

9. When and where have you been discouraged to use your voice? Where has permission been withdrawn?

Whose permission do you actually need to fulfill your ministry? This is a literal question. Whose permission do you need to use your voice, *your* voice? The persons or entities whose permission you actually need might be different from the persons or entities that have given permission in the past or that are currently in your head talking to you. Make a list of those whose permission you need to use your voice in ministry, to speak, to preach, to lead in worship. There is a soft kind of permission, those whose approval in relationship you want. And then there is the more firm permission, the technical, the ecclesial permission. In my Presbyterian and Reformed tradition, I need the call and approval of the Presbytery and the call of the church to fulfill an ordained position. I do not need the permission of my father or mother (though, in reality, some women do); I do not need the permission of a spouse (though, in reality, some women do).

The relational permission, the approval of those around you, is often the hardest to get. You might be on a church staff, but the head of staff never puts you into the preaching rotation. You might feel strongly called and affirmed outside your family, but the family tradition does not easily permit you to follow that call, as in Chatty Cathy's case. Sit down and think through these persons and entities and figure out whose permission you really need to use your voice in ministry.

It might be that you have been encouraged to use your voice, but only in roles approved for women: teaching children and youth, doing pastoral care with women and perhaps the elderly, or music ministries. Do you feel called to use your voice in ministries that are discouraged for women? Think it through. Make the list.

Where and how have you been discouraged to use your voice? Conduct the same exercise. Where and when has permission been withdrawn, or never granted in the first place? Who are the parties involved? These may not be pleasant experiences or dimensions of your life to visit. But it is important in claiming your own voice to be aware of who would hold you back. When we have been called by God and have been confirmed by a community of faith in that call, we need to be perceptive about who would bind us from following that call and to disempower that person, persons, or entities. Often they hold more power in our head and heart and spirit than they actually do in reality.

The function of this exercise is to get women thinking about the dynamics that have affected their voices. Typically we spend a good while talking about these things before we ever get down to actual voice work. A cohort of four to six women is optimum for mutual support, for having others to listen to, to learn passively from the feedback given to others, and to have the opportunity, each one, to get up and speak with sufficient frequency to carry lessons learned from one session to the next.

Body Work: Voice as a Full-Body Instrument

Breathing is to speaking as water is to a fish. No one can speak without breathing. Many basic vocal issues can be resolved simply by learning how to breathe. When we are born, assuming a baseline of good health, we know how to breathe. We breathe the way God designed us to breathe. As time goes on and we experience stressors and hear "No!" and begin to become self-conscious, our tendency is to breathe in a more shallow fashion.

Kristin Linklater is one of the leading voice specialists in the country. Her method and efforts are focused on "freeing the natural voice."[3] The method is based on the fundamental assumption that our God-made, natural ability to breathe, and the voice that is fueled by that breath, gets interrupted. The interruption comes when we are first corrected for how and when we use our uninhibited voices and when as a baby our natural crying out no longer gets us what we need. When a toddler's crying and kicking is no longer rewarded with something to eat, but rather nice and polite behavior is required (please and thank you), the natural impulse to respond from the gut is restricted. The "please and thank you" come from a place of intentional control, higher in the chest, and perhaps even with higher pitch. The spontaneous crying out for what we need is restricted and regulated so that we can develop appropriate control.[4]

Of course, to get along in human society we need some forms of modification, regulation, and control over the baby's instinctive cry when the baby is hungry or needs a diaper change. We cannot go through life screaming to get what we want. But that spontaneous voice that comes from our core, our gut, our abdomen, needs to be available to us. That spontaneous voice with deep and relaxed breathing is often not available to the women with whom I work.

The exercises that follow are my adaptations of exercises I have learned at the Linklater Center for Voice and Language. These exercises are only a fraction of what the reader will find in Linklater's book or in work with a designated Linklater teacher. I find these exercises helpful, however, especially for those who have never done body work *for the sake of their voices.*

You may have done the following exercise, or something like it, in an exercise class or for relaxation purposes. We are doing it with particular attention to how it matters for speaking. Each exercise as presented below can be done in one to two minutes, though the more time you spend and the more often you repeat the exercise, the more beneficial you will find the work. To the extent possible, do the exercises in comfortable clothing, wearing no shoes, and at a time and place where you will not be interrupted. Alternatively, if locking your office door for ten minutes and simply taking off your shoes is the only way you can get this done, then do it! Loosen any clothing that is binding. Once again, we are making connections to our bodies and to our breath for the sake of our voices. If any position or exercise is difficult, painful, or impossible, find the position that best suits your body's needs and enables you to accomplish the end goal of the exercise.[5]

EXERCISE 5A Floor At-Rest Posture

- Lie down on the floor on your back; be comfortable: comfortable clothing, no shoes, perhaps on a towel or mat. If getting down on the floor is not possible or comfortable, do this on a bed or on as firm a surface as possible.
- Elongate your body; stretch from your feet to your head.
- Draw your knees toward your chest to stretch your back.
- Keeping your shoulders on the floor, you might roll your knees from side to side, stretching out the sides of your back.
- Lower your legs back to the floor, seeking to remain long and keeping the small of your back as close to the floor as is possible and comfortable.
- You may want or need to bring your feet up slightly so that the bottoms of your feet are flat on the floor rather than on your heels. Do not draw your knees up tightly to your midsection.
- Stretch out your arms at your sides at about a 45° angle, with your hands in a neutral, non-effortful position. This will probably mean that the outsides of your hands are resting on the floor.
- Adapt the position as needed for comfort.
- Breathe.

What we are seeking to do here is to find a neutral position on our backs that creates no stress or strain on our skeletal or muscular structures. You may think this is simple or obvious or easy. In some ways it is. Most of us are able to lie on our backs. You will probably find, however, that completely relaxing into the floor is difficult to do. Most typically, we carry tension in our shoulders, neck, and hips and continue to do so even when we go to bed. We have to tell ourselves to relax. We have to send the message to our bodies to let go. If you have trouble falling asleep, try telling yourself to sink into the bed and pillow and let go of the tension in your shoulders and hips. When I do this I find I have been holding myself up off the bed. I tell myself to let go, to relax my shoulders and neck, and I literally sink lower into the bed. That is what we are seeking to do here. Relax into the floor. You do not have to hold yourself up. The floor will hold you.

EXERCISE 5B Feeling the Belly Breath
- Shut your eyes, relax, and breathe; pay attention to your breath.
- Slow down your breathing as you release tension and control.
- Slow down your breathing by inhaling through your nose for a slow count of six; hold your breath for a slow count of two; exhale through your mouth for a slow count of eight.
- Once your breathing has slowed down, breathe naturally.
- Make minor adjustments in posture for comfort.
- Breathe; be in this position for several minutes.
- Now while barely moving your elbows, place your hands on the sides of your abdomen, on your ribcage so that your hands are resting lightly on your ribcage. Make sure your hands are not on top of your abdomen and that your fingers are not laced together.
- Breathe.
- Begin to note the rise and fall of your belly as you breathe. This is good! Allow your belly to rise and fall naturally as you breathe.
- After several breaths, feeling your belly rise and fall, take a slightly deeper breath and let it out slowly, and then go back to natural breathing. Do this several times.

We are conditioned from an early age to hold in our stomachs. We hold in our stomachs for good posture, to enable us to stand erect, and to maintain good core strength. We also hold in our stomachs to look smaller and to fit into smaller clothing. It takes a lot of practice to maintain good body posture and core strength and to have relaxed bellies for breathing. Right now we are trying to get comfortable with relaxed bellies for breathing. We do this on the floor where good posture takes no muscular or skeletal effort, and where the rise and fall of our bellies is seen by no one except, perhaps, by an instructor who is looking to make sure our bellies are rising and falling!

When we rest our hands lightly on our abdomen, arms completely relaxed, we can feel the rise and fall of our bellies when we breathe. We should make no effort to control or regulate our breathing beyond the conscious effort to slow down our breathing, which is part of relaxing. We are seeking to let our bodies breathe the way they were designed. As you experience the rise and fall of your belly while breathing, *make this connection*:

When your belly rises, you are inhaling.
When your belly falls, you are exhaling.

Do not try to change this! This is correct. When you are lying on your back and you inhale, your belly rises. When you exhale, your belly falls. By the time this book is published, my beloved Bichon, Buddy, will be fifteen years old. He is doing great. But he sleeps so soundly during the day that I often look at his belly to make sure he is breathing. I hope that when it is his time to go, he goes quietly in his sleep. In the meantime, I am always relieved to see his midsection expand as he breathes. Yes, dogs too; this is the way God designed us.

If you are a trained vocalist or a musician who plays a wind instrument, these exercises and ideas are familiar. In fact, they are your stock-in-trade. Why is it often so difficult, then, for singers to maintain these disciplines when speaking? Thinking back to Chatty Cathy, we see that there is more going on when we speak than simple mechanics. Self-understanding, content, hearers, context, living into our bodies, loving our bodies—*as women*—these all influence how we use our voices. The person who feels comfortable singing and knows how to use the full-body instrument may have significant apprehension about the purpose for which the speaking voice is being used. The instrument, however, is the same.

When your belly rises, you are inhaling.
When your belly falls, you are exhaling.

Probably no one reading this book has not had the experience of "sucking in the belly" when trying on slacks or a skirt that are a bit too small. The classic example is trying on a pair of jeans that is one size too small and taking a deep breath to suck in the belly in order to zip up and button the jeans. When we take that kind of deep breath, we contract the abdominal muscles, lift our chest and shoulders, and fill our upper-chest cavity with air. This simple procedure has helped to train many women that taking a deep breath means pulling the belly in and expanding the upper-chest area. This is called upper-chest breathing. It is the opposite of the way we were designed to breathe. So difficult is it to correct this habitual misunderstanding that it is best to experience proper breathing on the floor, on our backs, in a trusted group with virtually no one watching, so that we can re-experience how the body behaves when it is breathing naturally and freely.

In the next two exercises, we are going to have a conscious experience of what happens when we create and hold tension in some of the major muscle groups. These are places where we are most likely to hold tension when standing to speak.

EXERCISE 5C **Contracting Gluteus Maximus on the Floor**
- Take a deep breath (sometimes known as a cleansing breath) and release it slowly; purse your lips almost into a whistle so that you can hear the slow and controlled release of breath.
- Go back to natural breathing rhythm.
- Put your hands back on floor with your arms at 45° away from your body.
- Contract the gluteus maximus muscles. These are the large

muscles that stretch across your buttocks. More plainly speaking, clench your buttocks muscles. Squeeze them tightly; that is, clench or contract them hard. Release. Do this a couple times.
- Note what happens to the posture of the body when you contract the "glutes."
- Repeat this clenching a couple times. Notice how hard it is to continue the natural belly breathing when you contract the glutes.

What happens when you tighten or contract your gluteus maximus muscles, your buttocks muscles? Your hips rise up off the ground. Your posture is changed. It is likely you stopped breathing when you did this. In fact, it is likely that contracting the glutes created tension throughout your body. Repeat Exercise 5C, noting the tension created throughout the body and how difficult it is to maintain relaxed, natural breathing.

EXERCISE 5D
Contracting Arms, Shoulders, Chest on the Floor
- After recovering a relaxed rhythm of belly breathing, take another deep breath and release it slowly. Continue relaxed belly breathing.
- Now clench your fists (your arms are still outstretched on the floor), contract the large muscles up your arms and across your chest, shoulders, and neck. These will be the muscles in the forearms, biceps, deltoids, pectorals, and trapezius muscles.
- Relax and unfold your fingers.
- Repeat the contraction of arm, shoulder, chest, and neck muscles.
- Note what happens to the posture of your body when you contract these large muscle groups.
- Repeat this exercise a couple of times. Notice how hard it is to continue the natural belly breathing when you contract these large muscle groups.

What happens when you contract the large muscle groups in your arms, chest, shoulders, and neck? What happens to your body posture? Your arms and shoulders literally rise up away from the floor;

Embodied Voice

they gain altitude as your hips did in the previous exercise. And again, it is likely you did not breathe when you contracted these muscles.

EXERCISE 5E Resume At-Rest Position
- Conclude this first set of exercises by going back to your at-rest original position on the floor as indicated in 5A.
- Find the relaxed posture, then draw your knees to your chest. Put your feet back on the floor; roll your knees to stretch the back; and then extend your legs again and breathe.
- Take a few cleansing breaths, releasing air slowly.
- Take two minutes or so for slow, relaxed belly breathing.
- Rise slowly off the floor, taking time for your blood pressure to equalize.

We have now had the experience of breathing properly in a totally relaxed position and posture. We have let the floor support us and have felt the relaxation when we sink into the floor. We have felt the natural rise and fall of our bellies as we inhale and exhale. No effort was required to breathe. There was no forced sucking of air to take in a breath and no pushing air out to exhale, except on the long, slow cleansing breath where we provided a little resistance to the exhale.

The goal now is to achieve the same thing in the upright position. If you need to do this from a seated position, seek an upright posture where your arms can hang at your sides or with hands relaxed on your legs. Your arms, however, should not be up on the armrests of the chair. Old habits are going to kick in immediately, so the following exercises are designed to teach you a new way to stand and a new way to approach a podium or lectern or music stand or pulpit. The first exercise asks you to "assume the default position." The default position needs to become your new resting place when you stand to speak.

EXERCISE 5F The Default Standing Position
- This exercise is best done in bare- or stocking-feet to feel connection to the floor, the base of support.
- Stand erect with the crown of your head held comfortably high.

- Make sure your shoulders are comfortably back, not hunched forward.
- Place your feet approximately eight inches apart.
- Put one foot very slightly forward, one foot slightly back with only about half an inch difference.
- Balance your weight evenly on both feet.
- Make sure your knees are relaxed, not locked.
- Hang your arms loosely at your sides.
- Stand there and breathe.
- Seek to breathe in the same relaxed fashion you did when you were on the floor.

The key to the default standing position is to have one foot slightly forward and one foot slightly back with the weight evenly distributed on both feet. Distributing the weight evenly on both feet may be natural, but most people will have their feet even with each other. When the feet are even with each other, it is much easier to lock the knees. When we lock the knees we are inclined to contract the hamstring, quadriceps, and gluteus maximus muscles. When we contract those muscles, we cut off our base of support, the bottom half of our bodies, and it is harder to move naturally, something we want to be able to do. When we lock the knees, it is also easier to sway reflexively, something we do not want to do. And as anyone who has ever been in a marching band, or in the military, or even in a wedding party may know, locking the knees can lead to fainting, especially on a hot day and when under pressure, because it constricts blood flow. Locking the knees cannot lead to any positive outcome when we stand to speak.

Get a feel for the new default standing position. Become acquainted with the relaxed, natural belly breathing in the default standing position. There should be no tension in your legs, arms, shoulders, or neck. Your hands should be hanging loosely at your sides. As much as possible, you want to experience the same kind of relaxed breathing you did on the floor. This is not a comfortable position for many people. Many people feel exposed and vulnerable in this position. Many feel as though their hands are awkward, as if the fingers are a bunch of bananas. The fact is that this default standing position is a perfectly natural position that does not draw attention to itself at all. For the purposes of our exercises, work at getting comfortable in this position. Later we will talk about other things you can do with your hands that will not interfere with your breathing. If it would help, place your hands lightly on the top of your belly, or on the sides of your abdomen, and feel the belly swell or expand as you inhale and deflate as you exhale.

Women tend to be self-conscious about their bellies expanding when breathing. Somewhere around adolescence we learned that the way to pull in our stomachs was to take a deep breath into our chests. This is a bad habit of backwards breathing. Taking in a breath should fill the belly with air. Filling the chest with air is called upper-chest breathing and will create a breathlessness usually caused by not fully exhaling the air we have already taken in.

Now that you have experienced natural belly breathing in the new default standing position, with no tension in the body, we will repeat the tension exercises we did on the floor, only in an old standing position. Note what happens to your posture and breathing when you do these exercises.

EXERCISE 5G   Standing with Body Tension
- Place your feet about eight inches apart and even with one another, that is, one foot is not slightly forward nor back. *This is not the new default standing position.*
- Contract your glutes, your buttocks muscles. Squeeze tightly for a couple seconds, then let go.
- Repeat. What is happening to your posture? Your breathing?
- Shake out your legs and resume the position with feet even with each other.
- Clench your fists, contracting your biceps, deltoids, pecs, and traps; squeeze tightly a couple seconds, then let go.
- Slowly relax and unfold your fingers.
- Repeat. What is happening to your posture? Your breathing?
- Shake out your whole body, release any remaining tension, and resume the new default position; breathe.

What happens when you contract the gluteus maximus? Your pelvis rotates out; your center of gravity shifts. It becomes difficult to breathe. You have effectively cut off your breath from your base of support. What happens when you contract the arm, shoulder, and chest muscles? Your shoulders rotate in, your neck becomes engaged and tense, and you really do not have access to belly breathing.

Most people stand with tension in their major muscle groups. This is unnecessary and inhibits natural belly breathing. We do not need to exercise the major muscle groups to stand. The major muscles that we have been contracting are working muscles. They do not need to work to enable us to stand. Small muscle groups and the skeletal structure are sufficient for standing. We need the major muscle groups for athletic activities and yard work and picking up heavy items and maybe pushing the vacuum cleaner. We need the major muscle groups for climbing stairs and even rising out of a chair. But we do not need the major muscle groups to stand in a relaxed position.

Most people stand with tension in one or more of their major muscle groups. You experienced how difficult it is to breathe when you contracted these muscles, both lying down and standing up. We have been engaging these large working muscle groups more intensely than you would in even the tensest speaking situations. But the exercise demonstrates what happens when you carry any tension at all in these parts of the body. Some people think that, behind a pulpit, it doesn't matter what you do with your feet, your legs, or even your arms and hands. I see preachers standing on one foot and tapping the toe of the other foot behind them. They have cut off the base of support for their full-body instrument. I see preachers clinging to the pulpit or grasping the sides of the pulpit. They are creating tension in the chest and shoulders and have cut off the base of support for their full-body instrument. I see preachers grasping the pulpit and leaning over it, and even wrangling it, or standing with elbows locked and shoulders hunched as they lean on it. They have cut off the base of support for their full-body instrument. These adverse body postures matter; they have a negative impact on the voice.

We will experiment with one final, common posture that creates problems in the use of our full-body instrument voices. This posture has to do with the way many of us were taught to stand "like a lady" when we were growing up and with the shoes we wear. Up to now we have been working barefoot or in socks. For this exercise, put on the shoes you are likely to wear in a public context of speaking.

EXERCISE 5H **Standing Like a Lady**
- Walk around the room in your shoes; walk in a relaxed fashion, seeking to continue your natural and relaxed belly breathing.
- Take the shoes off and walk again; experience the difference in posture, especially if you were in heels.
- Repeat: Walk without shoes, and then with shoes.
- Another way to do this exercise is to be without shoes, but rise up on the balls of your feet as though you are in heels; feel the tension in your legs and buttocks.
- With shoes on, place your feet together, heels nearly touching and toes extending out to create a 45° angle with your feet. This is the ballet first position. You might have one foot slightly forward, and that knee might be slightly bent.
- What do you notice happening in your legs and hips?
- Repeat the exercise: move from the new default standing position with feet about eight inches apart and one foot slightly forward, one foot slightly back, to the ballet first position with heels together and toes pointed outward to create the 45° angle.

It is likely that if your shoes have greater than one-inch heels, you felt tension in your legs, knees, and hips when you stood and walked in your shoes. This is especially true in comparison to what it feels like to have your feet directly connected to the floor. When you put your heels together, which means your knees were together, it is likely that your knees locked. When our knees lock, we create tension all up and down our legs and into our hips.

Many of my women have difficulty standing with their feet apart. They simply were not taught to stand that way. In fact they were taught precisely not to stand that way. It is indelicate, not feminine; it opens the legs in a manner they were taught is suggestive and inappropriate. When they were taught how to stand, however, there was no thought given to using their voices, and certainly not using their full bodies as the engine and base of support for those voices.

I am a sports fan, which means I watch ESPN. I have noted that the women who are now featured sportscasters on ESPN have adopted a new pose that would not have received approval when I was growing up. These are athletic-looking women who are usually wearing form-fitting dresses that are sleeveless (the better to show off the fitness and toning of their bodies) and high heels. These women do *not* stand with their feet and legs together. In fact, they stand with their feet at least ten inches apart and their knees apart. It almost looks like they are expanding their shapely hips to fill the space they have. This is not a demure posture; it is an assertive posture. Note I say assertive, not aggressive. It is a posture that says, "I am holding my own. I have a right to be here. I am claiming my space." These women do not all have great voices, but neither do all the men have great voices. What the women do have is a claim to the space on the set that they are occupying, a set that has been a traditionally male space.

The posture I am advocating for speaking is counterintuitive to the way many women were raised and the way many pose for pictures. Many reading this book were taught to keep their knees together and their feet close together in a first-position ballet pose, with perhaps one foot in front of the other. Perhaps most of the weight is on the back foot with one foot and knee forward, a kind of "Miss America" pose. This is fine for contexts that don't involve public speaking, but it simply does not work adequately for vocal production.

We now have a new default standing position. What do we do with our hands? I have cautioned you not to grip the sides of the lectern or pulpit, not to lean into the pulpit so that it is holding you up, and not to hunch your shoulders over the pulpit. What do you do with your hands? Following is a set of alternative positions for the hands that creates ease of movement and natural gesture and keeps the body in a relaxed, neutral position. These hand positions will mitigate our tendency to grip the sides of the lectern surface or the sides of the pulpit. As we have seen above, gripping the sides of the lectern leads to tension through the arms and across the chest and shoulders. Gripping the sides of the lectern also makes a natural gesture more difficult. People who are gripping the sides of the lectern have a tendency to leave the palm of the hand on the lectern and simply wave with their fingers; they lift the finger away from the side of the lectern. This happens because their hands are stuck there. The hand positions offered below not only lead to a neutral and relaxed body position for speaking, but free us up for more natural gestures.

EXERCISE 51   **Hand Positions**
- Assume the default standing position behind a lectern, pulpit, or music stand, arms hanging naturally at your sides, hands relaxed.
- Place one hand in a relaxed fashion on the surface of the lectern, not on the side. Your fingers are not wrapped around the sides of the lectern.
- Lift the hand and gesture to the side.
- Bring the hand back to the surface of lectern.
- Let the hand slide down until the palm is off the lectern and the fingers are on the lip of the lectern, as if your hand is hanging off the bottom lip of the lectern, but with no significant weight on your fingers.
- Lift the hand and make a gesture as if for emphasis.
- You are in the default standing position, with one foot slightly forward. With the forward foot, take a small step back; now the other foot is forward.
- Bring your hands together in front of your navel; place one hand lightly in the other with both palms up and arms remaining relaxed.
- From this position, gesture with both hands and arms outstretched as if including everyone in a thought.
- Bring hands back in front with one hand in the other, both palms up.

The purpose of these exercises is to experience the full-body instrument in the way God intended it to be used. We have experimented with relaxed posture with abdominal or belly breathing in the way God designed us. Watch a healthy baby breathe when asleep. That's how we breathe when we are asleep, but we tend to change that in our waking hours as we grow and experience fear, anxiety, or self-consciousness or when we have been mistreated. Constricted breathing is a response to feeling vulnerable. Open, natural belly breathing reflects openness to the world. It requires a willingness to take up space and to claim the space we take. This openness of our bodies requires a willingness to be vulnerable to our hearers. When we find ourselves unable to do this, we will want to ask ourselves why. Once we know why, we will want to seek the healing, support, and education we need in order to give ourselves more fully to the work to which God has called us.

When women shrink in an effort to take up less space in the pulpit or other public contexts of speaking, they are constricting and shrinking the engine that powers vocal production. There are psychological and emotional dimensions involved in this tendency to shrink from the vocal task, which is why it is helpful to do these exercises in the context of other women.

The Private-Public Dimensions of the Voice

One form of pushback I receive from those who do not make a sound big enough to fill a room is the claim that doing so does not reflect who they are. A student will claim that producing more sound is incongruent with her personality. Some students are afraid that if they begin to create more sound, their people back home won't recognize them or will think seminary changed them or that they are putting on airs or trying to sound like the proverbial preacher by using a "preacher's voice." This proverbial preacher's voice is typically lower in pitch range with more round, sonorous sounds than is natural or authentic to the speaker. Some of my students are worried that if they create more sound, they will feel as though they are yelling.

In the past, some voice teachers might have encouraged a student to throw the voice to the back wall of the room, or to imagine the sound bouncing off the back wall. I find that women do not respond to this image very well. Throwing your sound at someone is not an inviting image. I encourage my students to think of their voices as a group hug. You would never have a group hug and leave someone out. Our voices need to include everyone in the room. To extend our voices to everyone in the room is an act of hospitality. Speaking up is extending ourselves to each person in the room; it is extending the good news to each person in the room. When they imagine it this way, most women would never want to leave anyone out.

How do we include everyone with our voice? Is it pushing more air? Is it yelling? To explain this dynamic, I use the spectrum of private to public dimensions of the voice. You would use the most private dimension of your voice speaking quietly to a beloved. It is not just your volume that changes, it is the tone and quality of the voice. If you need to yell to a child, "STOP!" because she is getting too close to a road, you instinctively employ the most public dimension of your voice. The voice is not just louder but resonates differently as well.

This is a spectrum; it is not an either/or. We can learn to blend the private and public dimensions of our voices to suit the occasion and the context.

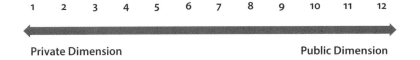

I suggested that the most private dimension of our voices, at number one on the spectrum, is suitably used when speaking privately and quietly to a beloved. I have referred to this as the pillow-talk voice. Move toward the public dimension, perhaps around number four on the spectrum, and you might hear in your head the old NPR voice. The vocal quality is velvety; the resonance comes from the back of the oral cavity, as though between the ears. In fact, when we resonate at the back of the oral cavity between the ears, our voices are very pleasing to our ears. Not only can we hear the velvet nature of the sound, we can feel it; we actually feel the resonance between our ears.

I suggested that the most public dimension of our voices is used when yelling. In order to produce this loud sound, we not only push more air, but we bring the resonance to the front of the face, what is called the front of the mask. Energy is literally felt more around the mouth and nose, chin, and cheeks. Perhaps the most public dimension of the voice is used when yelling to a child who is about to run into a street after a ball, or even screaming at a ball game. These would be a number twelve on the spectrum. Move toward the private dimension on the spectrum, perhaps to nine or ten, and imagine you are leading a worship service outside without the benefit of an amplification system. You won't be screaming; you will be seeking better vocal quality than there is in a yell or a scream. The volume will be high, however, and the resonance will come at the front of the face.

Sometimes the blend is tricky. For example, imagine you are conducting a wedding in a sizeable sanctuary and the sound system goes out. You have a bride and groom right in front of you and toward whom some of your words are exclusively directed, as when giving them the vows. Other words are for the congregation. You don't want to yell right into the faces of the bride and groom, but neither do you want to speak in a low-volume voice with a more private dimension when you ask those gathered if they will support the bride and groom in their new covenant relationship. To be sure, some will yell the whole service, not realizing how unpleasant it is for the wedding party, and some will speak in a casual, conversational tone, not realizing that only the wedding party and the first few rows of people can hear. We can do better than that. We can learn not only to listen and adjust the volume; we can also learn to tune our vocal production to private and public dimensions.

I have found that it is more helpful to talk about the private and public dimensions of the voice than it is to talk about volume when I am working with women. Usually they make a larger sound when thinking about using the public dimension, even if the volume is not raised. This approach helps us not to feel like we are being untrue to ourselves; that is, we can still feel in character.

I have had a few women in my teaching career who needed to work on using the private dimension of their voices; the public dimension came through virtually all the time. This is the friend with whom you are dining in a restaurant and whose voice is clearly reaching everyone who is sitting near your table. This is not just a volume issue; it is usually a private-public dimensions blend issue. It is more usually the case, however, that women need to work on the public dimension of their voices; they are often reluctant to sound aggressive when they are only being assertive, or are sometimes even reluctant to be heard at all.

Conclusion

In this chapter we have been talking about the embodied voice, and we have demonstrated some exercises that will lead us toward the use of the embodied voice. Everything we have done in the book thus far has been leading up to this. The use of the embodied voice, employing the full-body instrument, enables the preacher to preach the Word of God with authenticity and with faithfulness to her own truth. In the last chapter, we will conduct an oral interpretation workshop on a passage of Scripture and then hear a sermon based on that interpretive work.

CHAPTER 6

As If It Matters

John 11:1–44

Jesus! If you had been here, my brother would not have died!
Jesus! If you had been here. If only you had been here.

Martha first, and then her sister Mary a little later, admonishes
Jesus. This is one of those places in Scripture where we learn that God
can handle the full range of human emotions, including our recrimination. And this time it is women who teach us this lesson.

In this last chapter we are going to try on our full-body instrument voices for size. Essentially this is a workshop in oral interpretation. In the world of speech communication in ministry, we believe
that the oral reading of the Word is an interpretation of the Word.[1]
The oral reading of the Word is not just a matter of getting it out
in front of people so that they have a preview of what the sermon
might be about. Many people read Scripture as though it was only a
perfunctory duty in order to get to the sermon, the important part.
That is to suggest, however, that the Word of God does not have its
own voice. When the Word is read in a perfunctory manner, or the
reader has simply not prepared the reading, the tacit suggestion is
that our words in the sermon are weightier than God's Word. The
interpretation of Scripture in sermon is core to Reformed worship.
I would simply ask, How can the Scripture be heard in the preacher's interpretive process if the preacher has never heard the Scripture

read aloud, if the preacher has not actually *heard* it? In order to hear the Scripture, we must lend it our voices.

Therefore, we will conduct an oral interpretation workshop on John 11. This is the kind of work I suggest be done whenever Scripture is to be read for the purposes of preaching, and whenever possible in other circumstances where Scripture is read. This is preparing the Scripture for reading. We have been preparing our voices for this work. While not all of us will have been able to claim our Voices, and not all of us are yet able to employ our full-body instruments, I ask you to give the following exercises the voice that you do have.

I have chosen John 11:1–44 for this work because of the many dynamics involved in Jesus' interaction with Martha and Mary. This is one of the most in-depth conversations Jesus has with women in the New Testament. Jesus has a little spat with his somewhat intrusive mother at the wedding at Cana in John 2. Jesus has a frank, culturally transgressive theological conversation with the Samaritan woman at the well in John 4. There are disturbing encounters with women, such as with the Syrophoenician woman whose daughter was possessed by a demon. Jesus was reluctant to heal her, apparently comparing the woman and her daughter to "dogs" (Mark 7:24–30). There are encouraging accounts of women's relationships to Jesus such as in Luke 8:1–3, where it is reported that women accompanied him on his journeys with his disciples and "provided for them out of their own resources" (Luke 8:3). There are heartwarming, barrier-breaking encounters such as with the woman with the flow of blood in Mark 5.

One of the unique features of Jesus' encounter with Martha and Mary in John 11 is that they argue with him from the perspective of already being in a familial kind of relationship with him. We know how close they are by the message they sent to him: "Lord, he whom you love is ill" (John 11:3). They recriminate, "Lord, if you had been here, my brother would not have died" (John 11:21, 32). They push back when Jesus commands the stone be moved from the burial cave, "Lord, already there is a stench because he has been dead four days" (John 11:39).

John 11 gives us the opportunity to try on our full-body instrument voices using a range of emotions we rarely express in reading

Scripture, preaching, or leading in worship. Try out these exercises not thinking about how you would do it in church. Let's pretend we are not in church yet. Our worshiping contexts often determine how much or little emotion is expected from us. Some of us are accustomed to reading or hearing every passage of Scripture read in the same way as every other passage of Scripture. Do the exercises as if you are in a retreat workshop setting, not in Sunday morning worship. Give yourself permission to explore with your voice. If you can do these exercises in the context of a small cohort of women, listening to each other, trying things out, encouraging and giving feedback to one another, all the better. Open your Bibles to John 11.

Oral Interpretation Workshop on John 11:1–44

Martha and Mary send a message to Jesus, "Lord, he whom you love is ill." Presumably they want and expect Jesus to come right away and to heal Lazarus. Jesus, however, delays. When he finally arrives in Bethany, the drama between Jesus and Martha and Mary begins. Imagine the possible emotions Martha and Mary are feeling at the death of their brother. Martha, the more active one, runs out to meet Jesus when she hears he is drawing near. Mary stays at home.

Lord, if you had been here, my brother would not have died.

What emotions can we imagine Martha feeling? She is hurt and let down, to be sure. Is she angry? Does she feel betrayed? Is Martha merely suggesting that maybe perhaps Jesus kinda shoulda coulda been there? Is she fearful to confront Jesus? Is she meek or bold? What was the level of Martha's expectation that Jesus arrive in time? What is the depth of relationship leading Mary and Martha to send word to Jesus that Lazarus was ill? What is the emotional tone of voice, what is the volume with which Martha says to Jesus, "Lord, if you had been here, my brother would not have died"? What might be the blend between the private and public dimensions of her voice?

EXERCISE 6A John 11:21
"Lord, if you had been here, my brother would not have died."

Vocalize the line with the following emotional tones and volume:

- Meek and unsure, reflection rises at the end, as if it's a question.
- Matter of fact statement, even tone, narrow pitch range.
- Quietly intense, trying to hold back tears and anger.
- Accusatory, more volume.
- Angry, loud, with bitter betrayal.
- Whiny with a lot of "dipthongs" (pitch moving within a word).
    Lo oo$_{oo}$rd!   dii$_e$ed
- Wailing in grief.
- Other emotional tones and volumes you can imagine.

Vocalizing out loud and listening to our own voices allows us to experiment with a range of emotional content. We accomplish that range through varying the pitch, rate, volume, and private-public dimensions of our voices. Trying on a range of expressions allows us to experiment with our own interpretation of the text. It allows us to experiment with our own emotional response to Jesus delaying when we need him. It emboldens us to speak our own truth. There is no truth to your statement if you speak it in the habitual rut of nice and kind when what you are feeling inside is anger and betrayal. There is no truth for you, and there will be no truth for your hearers.

The line "Lord, if you had been here, my brother would not have died" is not spoken in isolation, however. Martha follows immediately with, "But even now I know God will give you whatever you ask of him" (John 11:22). Martha's brother Lazarus is dead. He has been buried. She is disturbed that Jesus did not arrive in time to heal Lazarus, to save him. "Lord, if you had been here, my brother would not have died" is more than a statement of fact. It is a kind of accusation, at least tinged with regret. Now Martha speaks this statement of apparent hope. "But even now, but even now …" What is the emotional content, what is the nature of faith embodied in those words?

We ask what is embodied because it is more than what lies behind the words. The truth is not behind the words; the truth is in the words as we speak them, as we feel them, as we embody them. And as we embody the words of the text, the Scripture points to a world envisioned by the text. The meaning lies not behind, but in front of the text as we give it voice.

EXERCISE 6B   John 11:22
"But even now I know God will give you whatever you ask of him."

Vocalize the line with the following emotional tones and volume:

- Resignation; you are humoring Jesus.
- Resignation; this is a creedal statement, appropriate at the moment.
- Feminine wiles, batting eyelashes, pleading, lower in volume.
- A hint of little-girl voice.
- A shred of hope.
- Boldly hoping Jesus can and will do the impossible, higher in volume.
- Daring Jesus to do the impossible.
- Other emotional tones and volumes you can imagine.

These two phrases together require we listen—and think as well, but really listen—through a complex set of emotions. Physically enact the scene. Run, or walk with deliberation, toward Jesus, your imagined Jesus in a specific place in the backyard or an isolated place in the park. Place yourself in the situation of having just lost a loved one when you know Jesus could have done something about it. What are you feeling? What does your voice sound like? What are your physical gestures? What are you hoping for?

We can guess, but not really know, what Martha was expecting. Surely there was a shred of hope when she said, "But even now I know God will give you whatever you ask of him." Even now, even though he is dead, perhaps there is still something Jesus can do. Is that what Martha might be thinking? It seems that Jesus' response disappoints. When Jesus says to Martha, "Your brother will rise again," Martha says, "I know that he will rise again in the resurrection on the last day" (John 11:23–24). Is Martha resigned to not seeing her brother until the last day? Is this a statement of faith? Is there an ellipsis at the end of the line, "at the last day . . ." as though she is waiting for more?

EXERCISE 6C **John 11:24**
"I know that he will rise again in the resurrection on the last day."

Vocalize the line with the following emotional tones and volume:

- Happy and relieved; this is just what you wanted to hear, higher in volume.
- Thoughtful, contemplative, lower in volume, thinking it through, asking yourself, "Is this what I believe?"
- Yeah, yeah, yeah, not pleased, a bit disrespectful; this is what everyone said to me in the funeral reception line.
- Disappointed; you didn't want to wait for the last day.
- Other emotional tones and volumes you can imagine.

We are focusing on the words of Martha, but we would be remiss not to consider the tone of Jesus' response. I have had students thump their chests with the palm of a hand when reading Jesus' response, "I am the resurrection and the life!" (John 11:25). We know what they are doing. They are providing contrast to Martha's interpretation of the resurrection. Martha doesn't have to wait for the last day. The resurrection is standing right in front of her. And in the presence of the resurrection there is life, not death. Less reflective readers also tend to miss the "I am" element of the statement. If a reader has not studied John and is not aware of the classic seven "I am" statements in the Gospel, nor how "I am" is reflective of God's answer to Moses, "Thus you shall say to the Israelites, 'I AM has sent me to you'" (Exod. 3:14), the reader is likely to put full emphasis on the "I" to the neglect of "I *am*." While this is a matter of interpretation for the purposes of any given sermon, the reader should at least be aware of the theological significance of the verbal construction, "I am." Also be aware of the different directions for a sermon these different renderings make available to the preacher.

What is Jesus' tone of voice in the "I am" speech? Is it a chest-thumping, prideful pronouncement? Is it an intellectual, theological correction? Is Jesus impatient or sympathetic?

EXERCISE 6D John 11:25-26
"I am the resurrection and life.
Those who believe in me, even though they die, will live,
and everyone who lives and believes in me will never die.
Do you believe this?"

Vocalize the line with the following emotional tones and volume:

- Emphasize "I" alone, deemphasizing "am," higher in volume.
- Emphasize both words, "I am," equally.
- The statement is a theological pronouncement—everyone take notes!
- The statement is a form of reassurance, a personal word to Martha, lower in volume.
- "Do you believe this?" as a challenge.
- "Do you believe this?" as encouraging a faithful response.
- Other emotional tones and volumes you can imagine.

Some preachers have only one way of reading this "I am" statement, and that is the way they read it at a funeral or memorial service. If this is the case with you, see if you can break the mold you have formed with this reading.

Martha's response to Jesus is affirmative. "Yes, Lord, I believe that you are the Messiah, the Son of God, the one coming into the world" (John 11:27). What is the possible range of emotions and faith with which Martha speaks these words? Does she feel chastised, encouraged, corrected, affirmed? Does she grasp what Jesus is saying?

EXERCISE 6E **John 11:27**
"Yes, Lord, I believe that you are the Messiah,
the Son of God, the one coming into the world."

Vocalize the line with the following emotional tones and volume:

- Relief; this is just what you wanted to hear, a little higher in volume.
- Intellectual assent, humoring Jesus, as if saying to yourself, "Okay, I'll say the right words," lower in volume.
- As if reciting a litany, an already well formed statement of faith.
- Disappointment; this is what everyone is saying to you, and Lazarus is still dead.
- Other emotional tones and volumes you can imagine.

Often we don't imagine for the purposes of reading how complex are the emotions involved in a story. In our rush to interpret the Scripture for preaching, or to move quickly to the Bible study, our tendency is to allow these characters to sound unidimensional. Perhaps Martha felt all of the above: relief that Jesus is the resurrection, disappointment that Lazarus will not be raised today, and some comfort in what might already be a kind of litany, a confession of faith. How would you read if you tried to imagine that whole complex of emotions going on at once? Isn't this the way we often feel in a time of crisis?

The scene moves from the edge of the village to the home of Martha and Mary. Martha ran out to meet Jesus. Mary stayed at home. When Martha went home and told Mary that Jesus was calling for her, Mary ran to where he was and fell at his feet. The verbal response of each sister is identical, even if initially one ran out to meet Jesus and the other stayed at home. Falling at the feet of Jesus, Mary says the same words as Martha, "Lord, if you had been here, my brother would not have died" (John 11:32). Repeat Exercise 6A. Revisit your work when you were speaking from Martha's point of view. Does Mary sound different? Does she express different emotions? Is there emotional content in this section other than what is represented in the exercise? What does it suggest about Mary's feelings or personality that she stayed at home while Martha ran out to greet Jesus?

EXERCISE 6F (a repeat of 6A only from
Mary's perspective) John 11:32
"Lord, if you had been here, my brother would not have died."

Vocalize the line with the following emotional tones and volume:

- Meek and unsure, reflection rises at the end, as if it's a question.
- Matter of fact statement, even tone, narrow pitch range.
- Quietly intense, trying to hold back tears and anger.
- Accusatory, more volume.
- Angry, loud, with bitter betrayal.
- Whiny with a lot of "dipthongs" (pitch moving within a word).
  Lo oo$_{oo}$rd!   dii$_e$ed
- Wailing in grief.
- Other emotional tones and volumes you can imagine.

The text does not report that Martha was weeping when she ran out to meet Jesus. Of course, that doesn't mean she was not weeping. But Mary's posture is described as decidedly different from Martha's. What does this say about the range of human emotion at such a grievous time?

When I ask students and workshop participants why Jesus cries when confronted with the weeping sister and mourners, the usual response is, "Jesus is weeping because he is sad; Lazarus is dead." This is possibly the case, though perhaps too simplistic. If Jesus was sad merely because Lazarus was dead, it would contradict his statement, "I am the resurrection and the life." Jesus went to Bethany knowing that what would happen there would be for the glory of God. Is he merely grieving the loss of Lazarus? Others suggest he is joining the grief of the sisters and their friends. Even though he knew he would raise Lazarus, he is crying to see them cry.

Why does Jesus weep? Why is he so deeply moved in spirit? Why is he so troubled? Perhaps Jesus is weeping at the sight of human grief, not just crying because they are crying, but weeping to see his beloved friends suffering so greatly. Perhaps Jesus weeps when we weep not because God cannot do anything about it, or because God merely sympathizes, but because he literally feels our pain. And even more, God feels the pain we suffer in light of our imperfect faith. We doubt the resurrection and the life when he is standing right in front of us. That must grieve God.

Karoline Lewis takes this one step further for us, which becomes important in our oral interpretation workshop. Lewis suggests that in the story of Jesus raising Lazarus from the dead, Jesus is brought face to face with his own death, the fullness of suffering that lay ahead because he was fully human. She suggests that "this moment is Jesus' 'agony in the garden' which is absent in the Fourth Gospel."[2] We might take up all these possible interpretations of what is going on when the Scripture reports that "Jesus wept." Whether you give more emphasis to one possible interpretation of Jesus' weeping than another, the oral interpreter has to confront the complexity of emotions that must be present: fear and hope, love and grief, and more.

The narrator of the story tells us that "When Jesus saw her [Mary] weeping, and the Jews who came with her also weeping, he was greatly disturbed in spirit and deeply moved. He said, 'Where have you laid him?' They said to him, 'Lord, come and see.' Jesus began to weep" (John 11:33-35). In some translations, verse 35 is simply, "Jesus wept." This section presents enormous challenges in oral interpretation for the reader and brings up the idea that besides the character voices, the reader has to settle on an authentic storyteller's voice, the narrator's voice. As the Scripture reader, you are the narrator; you lend your voice to the characters. How will you report to your hearers that Jesus wept? Where does that come from in your own heart and soul, your own gut, your own body? What is the tone, the inflection, the facial expression?

If we thought Martha had a shred of hope that Jesus would do something right here and now to bring Lazarus back from the dead, we see in the next scene how complex and inadequate human hope can be. Jesus asks that the stone be moved away (John 11:39). Martha does not respond with eager anticipation as though this is exactly what she hoped for; rather, Martha protests. There is nothing anyone can do about a decaying body. Don't even try. Was Martha hopeful when she said, "But even now I know that God will give you whatever you ask of him" (John 11:22)? What was she thinking God could do if Jesus would only ask? Apparently she wasn't hoping God would raise Lazarus, because now she protests that it is too late.

What we have done in the exercises above is a close reading of the text for oral interpretation. If you take this much time to prepare a hearing of the story, you will hear the questions that arise about the possible meanings of the story and the ways the story speaks to our contemporary situation. You will hear the complex nature of conviction, that it is never perfect. You will hear the agony of God in Jesus' tears. What we have done in the oral interpretive workshop is to demonstrate that the embodiment of the Scripture, the seeking to match the Truth of the Scripture with what we understand as the experience of our own truth, allowing the Scripture to reverberate inside of us, is as critical to the interpretation of the passage as all the critical study tools we learned in our exegesis classes. This is a lot of work. It takes a lot of time. But it is authentic. It allows the Scripture to actually speak, and to speak through us, through our bodying forth.

Following is the full text of John 11:1-44. The text is laid out on the page and formatted for oral interpretation. The formatting itself guides my reading of the text. Character speeches, the quotes, are in italics. This formatting makes the movement of the story clear to my eye as I read, delineating the character speeches from the narration. I make choices about direct and indirect eye contact based on whether I am in a narrative part or a character speech. I do this with all Scripture texts that I read in worship, and my sermons are also formatted this way to a great extent. If my sermon defies breaking it up into shorter paragraphs, or there is no place for a line break, then I know it isn't written for the ear. Long sentences and paragraphs are best suited for the eye, for reading quietly to oneself. Writing for the ear includes shorter phrases, repetition, and the use of parallel construction.

John 11:1–44

Now a certain man was ill, Lazarus of Bethany,
  the village of Mary and her sister Martha.
    ²Mary was the one who anointed the Lord with perfume
      and wiped his feet with her hair,
        her brother Lazarus was ill.
    ³So the sisters sent a message to Jesus,
  "Lord, he whom you love is ill."
⁴But when Jesus heard it, he said,
  "This illness does not lead to death;
    rather, it is for God's glory,
    so that the Son of God may be glorified through it."
⁵Accordingly, though Jesus loved Martha and her sister and Lazarus,
  after having heard that Lazarus was ill,
    he stayed two days longer in the place where he was.
⁷Then after this he said to the disciples,
  "Let us go into Judea again."
⁸The disciples said to him,
  "Rabbi, the Jews were just now trying to stone you,
    and are you going there again?"
⁹Jesus answered,
  "Are there not twelve hours of daylight?
    Those who walk during the day do not stumble,
      because they see the light of this world.
¹⁰*But those who walk at night stumble,*
  because the light is not in them."
¹¹After saying this, he told them,
  "Our friend Lazarus has fallen asleep,
    but I am going there to awaken him."
¹²The disciples said to him,
  "Lord, if he has fallen asleep, he will be all right."
¹³Jesus, however, had been speaking about his death,
  but they thought he was referring merely to sleep.
¹⁴Then Jesus told them plainly,
  "Lazarus is dead.

[15]*For your sake I am glad I was not there,*
so that you may believe.
But let us go to him."
[16]Thomas, who was called the Twin, said to his fellow disciples,
"Let us also go, that we may die with him."
[17]When Jesus arrived,
he found that Lazarus had already been in the tomb four days.
[18]Now Bethany was near Jerusalem, some two miles away,
[19]and many of the Jews had come to Martha and Mary
to console them about their brother.
[20]When Martha heard that Jesus was coming,
she went and met him, while Mary stayed at home.
[21]Martha said to Jesus,
"Lord, if you had been here, my brother would not have died.
[22]*But even now I know that God will give you*
whatever you ask of him."
[23]Jesus said to her,
"Your brother will rise again."
[24]Martha said to him,
"I know that he will rise again in the resurrection on the last day."
[25]Jesus said to her,
"I am the resurrection and the life.
Those who believe in me, even though they die, will live,
[26]*and everyone who lives and believes in me will never die.*
Do you believe this?"
[27]She said to him,
"Yes, Lord, I believe that you are the Messiah, the Son of God,
the one coming into the world."
[28]When she had said this, she went back and called her sister Mary,
and told her privately,
"The Teacher is here and is calling for you."
[29]And when she heard it, she got up quickly and went to him.
[30]Now Jesus had not yet come to the village,
but was still at the place where Martha had met him.
[31]The Jews who were with her in the house, consoling her,
saw Mary get up quickly and go out.

They followed her
    because they thought that she was going to the tomb
        to weep there.
³²When Mary came where Jesus was and saw him,
    she knelt at his feet and said to him,
    "Lord, if you had been here, my brother would not have died."
³³When Jesus saw her weeping,
    and the Jews who came with her also weeping,
        he was greatly disturbed in spirit and deeply moved.
    ³⁴He said,
    "Where have you laid him?"
They said to him,
    "Lord, come and see."
³⁵Jesus began to weep. ³⁶So the Jews said,
    "See how he loved him!"
³⁷But some of them said,
    "Could not he who opened the eyes of the blind man
have kept this man from dying?"
³⁸Then Jesus, again greatly disturbed, came to the tomb.
    It was a cave, and a stone was lying against it.
        ³⁹Jesus said,
    "Take away the stone."
Martha, the sister of the dead man, said to him,
    "Lord, already there is a stench
        because he has been dead four days."
⁴⁰Jesus said to her,
    "Did I not tell you that if you believed,
        you would see the glory of God?"
⁴¹So they took away the stone.
    And Jesus looked upward and said,
    "Father, I thank you for having heard me.
        ⁴²*I knew that you always hear me,*
        but I have said this for the sake of the crowd standing here,
        so that they may believe that you sent me."
⁴³When he had said this, he cried with a loud voice,
    "Lazarus, come out!"

⁴⁴The dead man came out,
    his hands and feet bound with strips of cloth,
      and his face wrapped in a cloth.
Jesus said to them,
    "*Unbind him, and let him go.*"

The following sermon, "As If It Matters," arises out of seeking to embody the words and truth of Martha and Mary and the complex of emotions, faith convictions, and cultural conditioning that led to their encounter with Jesus. Martha and Mary are models for us in the ways they each embody their own truth. We all know one who would rush out to Jesus, pouring out her feelings. And we all know one who would stay home and wait, but be no less passionate about her disappointment and grief. The mix of grief and hope, of faith and disbelief, of challenging authority and then acquiescing is a dynamic familiar to all of us. Seeking to embody the words of the sisters, to match what we understand to be true about our own experience with what may have been their experience, is key to interpreting the passage.

The subject and goal of the sermon, or the focus and function, are not about women's truth or women's bodies, or specifically the things that silence women. Rather, the sermon is launched from the platform of embracing these women, hearing what they have to say, and then testifying to who Jesus is in the midst of a grievous human loss. The tentative faith of Martha, "Yes, Lord, I believe you are the Messiah, the Son of God, the one coming into the world," is confirmed in the raising of Lazarus. We want to give voice to tentative faith and then confirm it in testifying not only to the resurrection, but the abundant life that is ours to be had in the present day.

As If It Matters

Jesus! If you had been here, my brother would not have died!
    Jesus! If you had been here. If only you had been here.
      If only you had been here, my life would be so different.
If only you had been here, I wouldn't have taken that awful job;

That fender bender would not have turned into a deadly car
crash;
If only you had been here I would not have lost my lover, lost my
parent, lost my baby ...
lost my spouse,
If only you had been here, my loved one would not be battling this
horrid cancer;
If only you had been here, I would know what to do with my life.
If only ... If only ... Fill in the blank.

If only Jesus would just be here! Get here on time. Come with his
power in his pocket and unleash it where we need it unleashed. We
know what we need. *Jesus* knows what we need. Just come and do it.
If you won't do it for us, the faithful, the prayerful, the hopeful, *your
friends*, then for whom?

If only you had been here.
When finally Martha gets the opportunity to fling these
words at Jesus,
she knows it is too late.
Lazarus is dead; dead and gone.
Buried in the tomb already for four days.
By this time he is rotting.
Surely even Jesus can't do much about that.
**"If only you had been here, Jesus, my brother would not have
died....
But even now I know that God will give you whatever you ask
of him."**
What is Martha saying? First she challenges Jesus, then she
retreats.
Martha gets angry with Jesus for not arriving in a timely manner
to help her beloved brother;
Martha is angry with Jesus for dilly-dallying when he could have
come sooner,
and then she apparently feels guilty for expressing her anger
because she immediately confesses.[3]

She immediately confesses that even in the face of her brother's
    death,
        she knows Jesus has this special relationship with God
            and God will do anything Jesus asks of God,
                and who is she to question Jesus or his actions or his
    motive?

Maybe, *maybe* there's a shred of hope beating in Martha's heart.
Perhaps there's a lingering thought that it's not too late. But probably
not. It is Martha after all who protests to Jesus later in the story, when
Jesus orders the stone removed from Lazarus's tomb, it is Martha
who protests.

Lazarus has been dead four days!
    His body is—oh, the maggots and worms—it's unthinkable!
    There will be a stench!
        Isn't it bad enough you didn't get here in time to heal him?
Surely you aren't going to denigrate his burial site by digging up
    a decaying body!
    He's dead! Leave him alone! Can't you leave us with this last
    dignity?
**"If only you had been here, Jesus, my brother would not have
    died....**
**But even now I know that God will give you whatever you ask
    of him."**
(As if *that* matters.)

And what does Jesus do? What does Jesus say? He trots out the same
tired litany Martha and Mary have been hearing from everyone else.

Empty, meaningless words for a moment such as this.
    "Your brother will rise again."
      As if it matters.

This is the teaching of the Pharisees. This they know. This is one
of those popular comfort phrases that people trot out at the time of

death to try and make the bereaved feel better. Your brother will rise again. You'll see him again in heaven. *As if it matters.*

Now friends, I'm sure you know by personal experience; I'm sure you know how inadequate you feel when you utter these kinds of words: **these clichés don't work.**

"Your brother will rise again."
"You'll see him again in heaven."
"You can always have another baby."
"You're young; you can get married again."
"It was his time."
"God needed another angel in heaven."
"This is just the way God chose to take him."
As if any of that matters—even if it's true!
You can't just explain away death, and you can't immunize against grief.
He's dead; it hurts; I have lost; and I just have to grieve.
And what do we get from Jesus? A pat answer. A cliché.
"Your brother will rise again."
As if that matters!

I am convinced that this is where most of us live. Honestly, day to day, we live in the personal knowledge that there is a God out there, but God doesn't deal very personally with us.

There is a God out there, but God doesn't seem to be tending to what is really going on or going wrong in life.

There is a God out there, but what good is that when the teenager is running wild,

or the spouse is running around with someone else,
or unemployment is running rampant and is your new way of life,
or we're caught in a state of intractable exhaustion caring for a sick child,
or elderly parents, or both children and parents at the same time,
or loneliness is your only and constant companion?

There is a God out there, but what good is that when we can't seem to find peace, or make peace or bring peace to the nations of the world?

There is a God out there, but what good is that when children are homeless and there have never been more refugees running from war and terror and starvation?

Your brother will rise again? I know, I know he will rise again, *as if it matters.*

A 2003 Gallup poll suggested that religious faith in this country is broad, but not deep. God is popular, but God is not first in many people's lives. "Belief in God" does not necessarily translate into "trust in God."[4]

I am convinced this is where many people are, even those of us who find ourselves in church every Sunday. We Americans are a religious bunch. It's part of what infuriates some of our neighbors around the world. We *are* a religious bunch. And even many Americans who aren't religious, apparently consider themselves spiritual. While the numbers have dropped a bit since 2003, still over half of Americans, 53 percent, say religion is important in their lives.[5]

But the gulf between belief and trust can be great. We go to church, more than nearly any other country in the world, we believe in God, some of us even read the Bible and pray. Those of us who are faithful church goers generally know the right answers. As a matter of fact, the churches that teach the right answers are the fastest growing churches in the country. We can recite the creed.

> I believe in God the Father almighty, maker of everything ...
> I believe in Jesus Christ, born of a virgin, suffered, died, was buried ...
>   raised again on the third day—yawn—sits up there in heaven with
>   God— hmmm, service is almost over.

But so what? So what? As if any of this really matters. What difference does it make?

- When the tragedies around the globe are so numerous and so horrible we have become accustomed to the horror;
- When there is political oppression and tyranny, war and terrorism in the Middle East and around the globe;

– When presidential politics have never been more absurd or
  ugly;
– When a typical family can hardly figure out how to run the family
  schedule and get everyone to where they're supposed to be;
– When we can't even protect our children in school, for crying
  out loud;

> *...from thence he will come to judge the living and the dead.*
>> So what? As if it matters!?!
> Martha responds with resignation.
>> "I know he will rise again in the resurrection on the last day."

Polite, confessional, nonconfrontational, another automatic
response. Is this Martha's truth? Does she immediately resign her
anger or bitterness or resentment that Jesus did not come sooner?

This is almost like a liturgical dance, a format to be followed at
the time of death. Folks go by in the receiving line and say the old,
familiar, presumably comforting words:

> "You'll see your brother again in the sweet by and by."
> "Oh thank you so very much; I feel much better now."

And then the bereaved go back home to weep in solitude so as not to
make anyone else feel too uncomfortable.

> Except, not this time. Not this time.
> **Our privilege, brothers and sisters, is that it is our job,**
>> **our vocation, our Monday-through-Sunday**
>>> **dawn-to-dusk duty to tell what happened next.**

> Jesus changed the tune.
>> He added a new verse.
>>> He broke wide open the ritual.

Can't you imagine the mourners hanging around, the disciples
hovering,

can't you see them all stop dead in their tracks,
a silence fall over them and all creation when Jesus spoke?
"*I am the resurrection and the life*," he said.
"*Those who believe in me, even though they die, will live,
and everyone who lives and believes in me will never die.*"

Martha stood in the very presence of the resurrection and could not comprehend the meaning of these words. She stood in the very presence of the resurrection and did not understand that not only in the sweet by and by, but now—there is life.

How much more difficult for us, for people in this age, for scientific, skeptical, starving, sick people to believe that the presence of Jesus is the very presence of the resurrected one, the very presence of the resurrection power of God; the resurrection from the dead, from hopelessness, from despair: the presence of life.

Our job is to tell this story. To tell the story as often and as convincingly as possible.

Our job is to live this story; to live out confidence in the resurrection.

Our job is not to be so distracted by church budgets and building-use policies and property disputes that we forget we are the manifestation of the risen Christ to the world.

Our job is to be consumed not by a concern for whether the church is ministering to us, but to be consumed by the Spirit of God with the desire to minister to the community and the world.

The resurrected one stands in our midst today, in the midst of grief and strife, of hopelessness
and despair, of war and fatigue and self-doubt.

The resurrected one stands in our midst today and says,

"*I am the resurrection and the life.
Those who believe in me, even though they die, will live,
and everyone who lives and believes in me will never die.
Do you believe this?*"

Our job is to work to the end that everyone, everyone knows and believes and trusts precisely this.

Our job is to work and witness to the end that everyone knows and believes and trusts that Jesus is the resurrection and the life and by the presence of the Holy Spirit works that resurrection power in every human hardship we endure.

We tell it *as if it matters*. Because it does. Nothing matters more.

Conclusion

I conclude with as much conviction about my thesis as I began.

> The voice is a full-body instrument.
> Many women struggle to speak.
> Many women struggle to speak because they are disconnected
> from their bodies.

We began this book by catching Miriam in the act of using her voice with her full body involved: bodily approaching and then speaking to power; spontaneously dancing and singing praises to God; voicing her righteous indignation and receiving the bodily punishment of leprosy; and then dying, leaving the Israelites in despair, in a place where there was no water. Miriam provides our biblical permission to use our voices, the mandate that the community of faith needs our voices, and the confidence that God's plan of salvation runs through the lives and voices of women.

We have looked at what kinds of life dynamics lead women to lose their voices and subsequently speak as though asking permission for the right to do so. Chatty Cathy was subject to gender norms in the church that restrict women from preaching; Sarah's experience of abuse left her disconnected from her body; Christine felt her personhood assaulted when, in a power play, a boss criticized her voice. We have found there are complex dynamics in the racial-ethnic and culture milieus from which we come. We have found that when women have not been given permission to speak or have not claimed the right to speak, the result is often a voice that is too high or too low in the pitch range, too low in volume to be heard, or that uses too much of a rise in inflection at the end of declarative sentences, what is known as upspeak, or that uses laughter as an apology for speaking with conviction.

We have examined why and how it is that women become disconnected from their bodies, and therefore from their full-body instruments. Cultural conditioning as to what size and shape constitutes the good body; the conditioning of girls to become nice and kind, calm and quiet, thereby disconnecting them from their own truth; and the reality of the physical and sexual abuse suffered by many women are all reasons why women disconnect from their bodies, either consciously or unconsciously.

We have looked at what it might take for women to claim our personhood and our own truth in order to body forth, literally to extend our body mass, all of it, to our hearers. We have gone through exercises to learn how to embody that voice and what physical activity is required in order to lend our bodies to the Word, to body forth.

Finally, we put all of this to work in an oral interpretation workshop on John 11, using our voices to experiment with possible emotions and tones expressed by Martha and Mary. We sought to match the truth of our own lived experience with the characters in the story, to resonate with their lived experience of grief and of faith.

The concluding word is that in our mutual calling to the gospel ministry, nothing matters more than embodying the Word of God. Women who are called to preach the gospel are called to use the voice they have been given, the female voice, the fully embodied voice. Whatever obstacles they face, whether they stem from lack of permission, from issues of abuse, from issues of body image, or from any other obstacle, I pray for all who read this book the courage to claim and use their full-body instrument in service to the church and for the sake of the reconciling ministry of Jesus Christ. Nothing matters more.

Notes

Notes to the Introduction

1. See Mary Donovan Turner and Mary Lin Hudson, *Saved from Silence: Finding Women's Voice in Preaching* (St. Louis: Chalice Press, 1999). This book addresses women's metaphorical Voice. See also Jennifer E. Copeland, *Feminine Registers: The Importance of Women's Voices for Christian Preaching* (Eugene, OR: Cascade Books, 2014).

2. See Noah Buchholz, "UMSL St. Louis Storytelling Festival 2012," accessed August 23, 2016, https://www.youtube.com/watch?v=Y2oN2Yo9aVI.

Notes to Chapter One

1. The third movement of a symphony is characterized as a scherzo, which technically means "joke." It is medium/fast and perhaps the lightest movement in tone.

2. I began working with these texts well over fourteen years ago. Eventually my research led me to an article by Phyllis Trible to which I am deeply indebted. Her article has been a conversation partner for me over these many years. Phyllis Trible, "Bringing Miriam Out of the Shadows," *Bible Review* 5, no. 1 (February 1989): 14–25, 34.

3. Renita J. Weems, *Just a Sister Away: A Womanist Vision of Women's Relationships in the Bible* (Philadelphia: Innisfree Press, 1988).

4. Trible, "Bringing Miriam," 18.

5. Trible, "Bringing Miriam," 19.

6. Trible, "Bringing Miriam," 19.

7. For a performance analysis of the Song of Miriam, see Mary Donovan Turner, "Reversal of Fortune: The Performance of a Prophet," in *Performance in Preaching*, ed. Jana Childers and Clayton J. Schmit (Grand Rapids: Baker Academic, 2008), 87–98.

8. Trible, "Bringing Miriam," 22–23.

9. Moses's obituary appears in Deuteronomy 34:1-12. Aaron's obituary is a mere

single verse; but at least it says that the whole house of Israel mourned him for thirty days. For Miriam there is simply a report that she died and was buried in the place where there was no water.

10. See Matt. 27:55-56; Mark 15:40-41; Luke 8:1-3.

Notes to Chapter Two

1. Gene L. Lowry, *How to Preach a Parable: Designs for Narrative Sermons* (Nashville: Abingdon, 1989).

2. There is not one monolithic Korean worshiping tradition any more than there is for any other demographic. I have taught Korean women with strong voices. See Eunjoo Mary Kim, *Women Preaching: Theology and Practice through the Ages* (Eugene, OR: Wipf and Stock, 2009), 118-56: "Korean Women Preachers during the Colonial and Post-Colonial Eras."

3. Won-Kyu Lee, *Honorifics and Politeness in Korean* (Ann Arbor, MI: University Microfilms International; Dissertation Information Service, 1993), 43.

4. Lee, *Honorifics and Politeness*, 68.

5. Lee, *Honorifics and Politeness*, 61.

6. It is outside the scope of this book to address the ordination practices of the various Protestant denominations found in the US. I have found it helpful, however, to keep an eye on the Women of Color in Ministry project (WOCIM) who are studying such issues as the number of women of color who are ordained, have installed positions in churches, have advanced degrees, and have regular faculty positions in higher education and the pay scales of women compared to men. These studies are focused on the experiences of women of color in pursuit of recognizing the talents and gifts of women of color and fairness with regard to such things as placement and remuneration in church organizations. See http://womenofcolorinministry.org/index.html.

Notes to Chapter Three

1. Emily Tess Katz, "Vocal Fry, Made Famous by Kim Kardashian, Is Making Young Women 'Less Hirable,'" *The Huffington Post*, November 3, 2014, http://www.huffingtonpost.com/2014/10/31/vocal-fry_n_6082220.html.

2. These figures are from a Center for Disease Control (CDC) summary, "Childhood Obesity Facts" (accessed February 17, 2016, http://www.cdc.gov/obesity/data/childhood.html), of a study by Cynthia L. Ogden, Margaret D. Carroll, Brian K. Kit, et al., "Prevalence of Childhood and Adult Obesity in the United States, 2011-2012," *Journal of the American Medical Association* (February 26, 2014), http://jama.jamanetwork.com/article.aspx?articleid=1832542. The category labeled "obese" is based on the Body Mass Index (BMI) approved by the CDC. For an alternative perspective on BMI from

that of the CDC, see Linda Bacon and Lucy Aphramor, *Body Respect: What Conventional Health Books Get Wrong, Leave Out, and Just Plain Fail to Understand about Weight* (Dallas: BenBella Books, 2014).

3. Eliana Dockterman, "Barbie's Got a New Body?" *Time*, February 8, 2016, http://time.com/barbie-new-body-cover-story/.

4. Margo Maine, *Body Wars: Making Peace with Women's Bodies* (Carlsbad, CA: Gürze Books, 2000).

5. Mimi Nichter and Nancy Vukovic, "Fat Talk," in *Many Mirrors: Body Image and Social Relations*, ed. N. Sault (New Brunswick, NJ: Rutgers University Press, 1994), 109–31. See also Analisa Arroyo, Chris Segrin, and Jake Harwood, "Appearance-Related Communication Mediates the Link between Self-Objectification and Health and Well-Being Outcomes," DOI: 10.1111/hcre.12036, International Communication Association Issue; *Human Communication Research* 40, no. 4 (October 2014): 463–82, http://onlinelibrary.wiley.com/doi/10.1111/hcre.12036/abstract.

6. Mimi Nichter, *Fat Talk: What Girls and Their Parents Say about Dieting* (Cambridge, MA: Harvard University Press, 2000). Interestingly enough, the dimensions of my copy of *Fat Talk* are unusually tall and slender. Most books that are nine inches high are at least five and three-quarters to six inches wide. My copy of *Fat Talk* is fully nine inches high and only four and three-quarter inches wide. The impact upon opening the package from Amazon was immediate. The book feels different in the hand; it reads differently as the eye is constantly moving down the page with little time spent going across the page; it is a constant visual illustration of tall and slender.

7. Maine, *Body Wars*, x.

8. Maine, *Body Wars*, 18.

9. Maine, *Body Wars*, 18, 292. I reference Maine's bibliography, which indicates studies cited.

10. Maine, *Body Wars*, 19.

11. Maine, *Body Wars*, 19, 292.

12. Joan Jacobs Brumberg, *The Body Project: An Intimate History of American Girls* (New York: Random House, 1997).

13. Brumberg, *The Body Project*, 22.

14. Brumberg, *The Body Project*, 43.

15. "Old Fashioned Weight Loss Ads," *The Huffington Post*, March 2012, http://www.huffingtonpost.com/2012/03/25/vintage-weight-loss ads_n_1373856.html#gallery/216538/9.

16. Brumberg, *The Body Project*, 99–118.

17. Brumberg, *The Body Project*, 108.

18. Brumberg, *The Body Project*, 112.

19. Nichter, *Fat Talk*, 51.

20. John Kell, "Lean Times for the Diet Industry," *Fortune*, May 22, 2015, http://fortune.com/2015/05/22/lean-times-for-the-diet-industry/. This article references studies done by Marketdata Enterprises.

21. Richard L. Cleland, Walter C. Gross, Laura D. Koss, Matthew Daynard, and Karen M. Muoio, "Weight Loss Advertising: An Analysis of Current Trends," A Federal Trade Commission Staff Report, September, 2002, https://www.ftc.gov/sites/default /files/documents/reports/weight-loss-advertisingan-analysis-current-trends/weight loss_0.pdf.

22. Kell, "Lean Times."

23. Margo Maine and Joe Kelly, *The Body Myth: Adult Women and the Pressure to Be Perfect* (Hoboken, NJ: John Wiley, 2005), 13.

24. Maine and Kelly, *Body Myth*, 13.

25. Maine and Kelly, *Body Myth*, 121–30.

26. Maine and Kelly, *Body Myth*, 5.

27. Two books I have found helpful in understanding better our bodies are Christiane Northrup, *Women's Bodies, Women's Wisdom: Creating Physical and Emotional Health and Healing* (New York: Bantam Books, 2002) and Deborah Sichel and Jean Watson Driscoll, *Women's Moods: What Every Woman Must Know about Hormones, the Brain and Emotional Health* (New York: William Morrow, 1999).

28. Lyn Mikel Brown and Carol Gilligan, *Meeting at the Crossroads: Women's Psychology and Girls' Development* (New York: Ballantine Books, 1992). See also Carol Gilligan, *In a Different Voice: Psychological Theory and Women's Development* (Cambridge, MA: Harvard University Press, 1982).

29. Brown and Gilligan, *Meeting at the Crossroads*, 21.

30. Brown and Gilligan, *Meeting at the Crossroads*, 22.

31. Brown and Gilligan, *Meeting at the Crossroads*, 12.

32. Brown and Gilligan, *Meeting at the Crossroads*, 53.

33. Brown and Gilligan, *Meeting at the Crossroads*, 91.

34. Brown and Gilligan, *Meeting at the Crossroads*, 108.

35. Brown and Gilligan, *Meeting at the Crossroads*, 170.

36. See also Rachel Simmons, *Odd Girl Out, Revised and Updated: The Hidden Culture of Aggression in Girls* (New York: Mariner Books, 2011).

37. Mary Pipher, *Reviving Ophelia: Saving the Selves of Adolescent Girls* (New York: Ballantine, 1994).

38. Erik Erikson, *Childhood and Society*, 2nd ed. (New York: W. W. Norton, 1979), especially 258–60.

39. Pipher, *Reviving Ophelia*, 17–26.

40. Pipher, *Reviving Ophelia*, 21–22.

41. For first-person stories of girls struggling with their identity, see Sara Shandler, *Ophelia Speaks: Adolescent Girls Write about Their Search for Self* (New York: Harper Perennial, 1999). See also Sharon Lamb and Lyn Mikel Brown, *Packaging Girlhood: Rescuing Our Daughters from Marketers' Schemes* (New York: St. Martin's Press, 2006).

42. There is a tremendous amount of discussion around whether the upspeak vocal inflection prominent in the speech of teenagers, especially females in the last twenty-five years or so, is the same as high rising tone (HRT) found in the speech

habits of whole cultures dating back as much as hundreds of years, for example in Australian English. For an introduction to this conversation, see Richard Nordquist, "Uptalk (high-rising terminal)," about education, November 27, 2015, http://grammar.about.com/od/tz/g/uptalkterm.htm, and Mark Liberman, "Uptalk Is Not HRT," *Language Log*, March 28, 2006, http://itre.cis.upenn.edu/~myl/languagelog/archives/002967.html. See also Sheryl Sandberg and Adam Grant, "Speaking While Female: Why Women Stay Quiet at Work," *New York Times Sunday Review*, January 12, 2015, http://www.nytimes.com/2015/01/11/opinion/sunday/speaking-while-female.html?_r=1: "We've both seen it happen again and again. When a woman speaks in a professional setting, she walks a tightrope. Either she's barely heard or she's judged as too aggressive."

43. Stanford victim of assault in Katie J. M. Baker, "Here Is the Powerful Letter the Stanford Victim Read Aloud to Her Attacker," BuzzFeed News, accessed July 27, 2016, https://www.buzzfeed.com/katiejmbaker/heres-the-powerful-letter-the-stanford-victim-read-to-her-ra?utm_term=.qe10ME5EA#.iwEPW3E3r. The entire letter the victim read in the courtroom is found at this website.

44. I identify the convicted rapist as the Stanford University swimmer as a way to identify the story, not because I think he is exceptional by virtue of his swimming prowess.

45. Baker, "Stanford Victim."

46. National Coalition Against Domestic Violence, "Domestic Violence National Statistics," accessed July 27, 2016, http://www.ncadv.org/files/National%20Statistics%20Domestic%20Violence%20NCADV.pdf.

47. Michele C. Black, Kathleen C. Basile, Matthew J. Breiding, Sharon G. Smith, Mikel L. Walters, Melissa T. Merrick, Jieru Chen, and Mark R. Stevens, "The National Intimate Partner and Sexual Violence Survey: 2010 Summary Report," http://www.cdc.gov/ViolencePrevention/pdf/NISVS_Report2010-a.pdf.

48. National Sexual Violence Resource Center, "Statistics about Sexual Violence," (2015), http://www.nsvrc.org/sites/default/files/publications_nsvrc_factsheet_media-packet_statistics-about-sexual-violence_0.pdf.

49. Justin S. Holcomb and Lindsey A. Holcomb, *Is It My Fault? Hope and Healing for Those Suffering Domestic Violence* (Chicago: Moody, 2014), 70.

50. The DSM-5 is the American Psychiatric Association's *Diagnostic and Statistical Manual of Mental Disorders*, 5th ed. (Arlington, VA: American Psychiatric Publishing, 2015). It is used to classify and diagnose mental disorders.

51. Daniel Sagalyn, "Army General Calls for Changing Name of PTSD," PBS *Newshour*, November 4, 2011, http://www.pbs.org/newshour/updates/military-july-dec11-stress_11-04/.

52. On the other hand, some experts claim that post-traumatic stress is a moderate condition where symptoms are less extreme and usually last no more than a month, therefore when it lasts longer it is a disorder. James Bender, "What Are the Differences between PTS and PTSD?" brainlinemilitary, accessed July 29, 2016, http://

www.brainlinemilitary.org/content/2013/12/what-are-the-difference-between-pts
-and-ptsd.html.

53. Diane Mandt Langberg, *Counseling Survivors of Sexual Abuse* (Wheaton, IL: Tyndale: 1997), 70–71.

54. Langberg, *Counseling Survivors*, 71–72.

55. Langberg, *Counseling Survivors*, 73–74. See also Susan Shooter, *How Survivors of Abuse Relate to God: The Authentic Spirituality of the Annihilated Soul* (Surrey, UK: Ashgate, 2012).

56. RAINN, "Perpetrators of Sexual Violence," accessed July 27, 2016, https://www
.rainn.org/statistics/perpetrators-sexual-violence.

Notes to Chapter Four

1. In his *Lectures on Preaching* at Yale University Divinity School in 1877, Phillips Brooks said that preaching has two essential elements: truth and personality. There is no other avenue through which the truth in preaching can come except for the personality of the preacher. We heard Christine in chapter 2 connect her voice to her personhood. We can claim the connection here of personhood-truth-voice.

2. The point of listing these Scripture references is to make a plea for greeting people in worship with the apostolic greeting, and not with a chirpy "Good morning!" It may very well not be a good morning for some, if not many, and being forced into a false chirpiness is not only annoying, it is contrary to the nature of God who beckons us and welcomes us in whatever broken state we find ourselves.

3. Alla Bozarth-Campbell, *The Word's Body: An Incarnational Aesthetic of Interpretation* (Tuscaloosa: University of Alabama Press, 1979), 31.

4. Wallace Bacon, *The Art of Interpretation*, 3rd ed. (New York: Holt, Rinehart, and Winston, 1979), 37–40. I will henceforth replace "poem" with "Scripture," even though in the world of performance studies, "poem" is the common name given to a piece to be interpreted.

5. Bacon, *Art of Interpretation*, 37.

6. Bozarth-Campbell, *Word's Body*, 31. Bozarth-Campbell states in her own footnote that "reverberation" was the subject of an unpublished typescript that was circulated among the faculty at Northwestern University for teaching purposes.

7. It is beyond the scope and purpose of this book to go into a review of performance studies and the discussion that swirls around the use of the words derived from "perform." The following book in honor of the work of my colleague, Charles L. Bartow, is a splendid resource on performance in preaching: Jana Childers and Clayton J. Schmit, *Performance in Preaching: Bringing the Sermon to Life* (Grand Rapids: Baker Academic, 2008).

8. "perform," Online Etymology Dictionary, accessed June 28, 2016, http://www
.etymonline.com/index.php?allowed_in_frame=0&search=perform.

9. For a fine discussion on the theology of sound, see Stephen H. Webb, *The Divine Voice: Christian Proclamation and the Theology of Sound* (Grand Rapids: Brazos, 2004), especially 13–55.

10. Surgery for voice feminization is available for transgender persons. See for example, "Voice Feminization," Center for the Care of the Professional Voice, accessed August 12, 2016, http://professionalvoice.org/feminization.aspx.

11. See, for example, Open Octave, "The Composer's Toolbox," accessed August 7, 2016, http://www.openoctave.org/the_composers_toolbox/orchestral_instruments /choir/soprano.

12. University of Iowa Voice-Academy, "Male and Female Voices," accessed August 7, 2016, https://uiowa.edu/voice-academy/male-female-voices.

13. See Joanna Cazden, *Everyday Voice Care: The Lifestyle Guide for Singers and Talkers* (Milwaukee: Hal Leonard, 2012), and C. Blake Simpson, "General Voice Care/Vocal Hygiene," UT Health Science Center (1996), accessed August 10, 2016, http://uthscsa .edu/oto/voice.asp.

Notes to Chapter Five

1. Dudley Knight, *Speaking with Skill: An Introduction to Knight-Thompson Speechwork* (London: Bloomsbury Methuen Drama, 2012).

2. See Daniel Lambroso and Olga Khazan, "The Science behind Hating Hillary Clinton's Voice," *The Atlantic*, Video, August 1, 2016; accessed December 12, 2016.

3. Kristin Linklater, *Freeing the Natural Voice* (Hollywood, CA: Drama Publishers, 2006).

4. See Linklater's famous "Chocolate Chip Cookie Story," *Freeing the Natural Voice*, 20–22. In this first section of the book, Linklater talks about why the voice does not work; and from her perspective, it is all about breathing.

5. See also Jana Childers, *Performing the Word: Preaching as Theatre* (Nashville: Abingdon, 1998), especially 57–77.

Notes to Chapter Six

1. There is no better resource for this consideration than Charles L. Bartow, *God's Human Speech: A Practical Theology of Proclamation* (Grand Rapids: Eerdmans, 1997).

2. Karoline Lewis, *John*, Fortress Biblical Preaching Commentaries (Minneapolis: Fortress, 2014), 158.

3. Raymond E. Brown, *The Gospel According to John I–XII*, The Anchor Bible 29 (New York: Doubleday, 1966), 432.

4. Helen T. Gray, "Soul-Searching Survey," *Knight Ridder Newspapers*, February 15, 2003, http://www.religionnewsblog.com/2383/soul-searching.

5. Angelina E. Theodorou, "Americans Are in the Middle of the Pack Globally When It Comes to Importance of Religion," Pew Research Center, December 23, 2015, http://www.pewresearch.org/fact-tank/2015/12/23/americans-are-in-the-middle-of -the-pack-globally-when-it-comes-to-importance-of-religion/.

Bibliography

American Psychiatric Association. *Diagnostic and Statistical Manual of Mental Disorders.* 5th ed. Arlington, VA: American Psychiatric Publishing, 2015.

Arroyo, Analisa, Chris Segrin, and Jake Harwood. "Appearance-Related Communication Mediates the Link between Self-Objectification and Health and Well-Being Outcomes." DOI: 10.1111/hcre.12036 International Communication Association Issue. *Human Communication Research* 40, no. 4 (October 2014): 463–82. http://onlinelibrary.wiley.com/doi/10.1111/hcre.12036/abstract.

Bacon, Linda, and Lucy Aphramor. *Body Respect: What Conventional Health Books Get Wrong, Leave Out, and Just Plain Fail to Understand about Weight.* Dallas: BenBella Books, 2014.

Bacon, Wallace A. *The Art of Interpretation.* 3rd ed. New York: Holt, Rinehart, and Winston, 1979.

Baker, Katie J. M., "Here Is the Powerful Letter the Stanford Victim Read Aloud to Her Attacker." BuzzFeed News. Accessed July 27, 2016. https://www.buzzfeed.com/katiejmbaker/heres-the-powerful-letter-the-stanford-victim-read-to-her-ra?utm_term=.qe1oME5EA#.iwEPW3E3r.

Bartow, Charles L. *God's Human Speech: A Practical Theology of Proclamation.* Grand Rapids: Eerdmans, 1997.

Belenky, Mary Field, Blythe McVicker Clinchy, Nancy Rule Goldberger, and J. Tarule. *Women's Ways of Knowing: The Development of Self, Voice and Mind.* New York: Basic Books, 1986.

Belleville, Linda L. *Women Leaders and the Church: Three Crucial Questions.* Grand Rapids: Baker, 2000.

Bender, James, "What Are the Differences between PTS and PTSD?" brainlinemilitary. Accessed July 29, 2016. http://www.brainlinemilitary.org/content/2013/12/what-are-the-difference-between-pts-and-ptsd.html.

Black, Michele C., Kathleen C. Basile, Matthew J. Breiding, Sharon G. Smith,

Bibliography

Mikel L. Walters, Melissa T. Merrick, Jieru Chen, and Mark R. Stevens. "The National Intimate Partner and Sexual Violence Survey: 2010 Summary Report." http://www.cdc.gov/ViolencePrevention/pdf/NISVS _Report2010-a.pdf.

Boone, Daniel R. *Is Your Voice Telling on You? How to Find and Use Your Natural Voice*. 2nd ed. San Diego: Singular Publishing, 1997.

Bozarth-Campbell, Alla. *The Word's Body: An Incarnational Aesthetic of Interpretation*. Tuscaloosa: University of Alabama Press, 1979.

Brooks, Phillips. *Lectures on Preaching*. New Haven: Yale University Divinity School, 1877.

Brown, Lyn Mikel, and Carol Gilligan. *Meeting at the Crossroads: Women's Psychology and Girls' Development*. New York: Ballantine, 1992.

Brown, Raymond. *The Gospel According to John I–XII*. The Anchor Bible Vol. 29. New York: Doubleday, 1966.

Brumberg, Joan Jacobs. *The Body Project: An Intimate History of American Girls*. New York: Random House, 1997.

Buchholz, Noah. "UMSL St. Louis Storytelling Festival 2012." YouTube. Accessed August 23, 2016. https://www.youtube.com/watch?v=Y2oN2Yo9a VI.

Cazden, Joanna. *Everyday Voice Care: The Lifestyle Guide for Singers and Talkers*. Milwaukee: Hal Leonard, 2012.

Centers for Disease Control and Prevention. "Childhood Obesity Facts." Accessed February 17, 2016. http://www.cdc.gov/obesity/data/childhood .html.

Childers, Jana. *Performing the Word: Preaching as Theatre*. Nashville: Abingdon, 1998.

Childers, Jana, and Clayton J. Schmit. *Performance in Preaching: Bringing the Sermon to Life*. Grand Rapids: Baker Academic, 2008.

Cleland, Richard L., Walter C. Gross, Laura D. Koss, Matthew Daynard, and Karen M. Muoio. "Weight Loss Advertising: An Analysis of Current Trends." Federal Trade Commission, September, 2002. https://www.ftc .gov/sites/default/files/documents/reports/weight-loss-advertising-an -analysis-current-trends/weightloss_0.pdf.

Copeland, Jennifer E. *Feminine Registers: The Importance of Women's Voices for Christian Preaching*. Eugene, OR: Cascade, 2014.

Cunningham, David S. *Faithful Persuasion: In Aid of a Rhetoric of Christian Theology*. Notre Dame and London: University of Notre Dame Press, 1990.

Dockterman, Eliana. "Barbie's Got a New Body?" *Time*, February 8, 2016. http://time.com/barbie-new-body-cover-story/.

Erikson, Erik. *Childhood and Society*. 2nd ed. New York: W. W. Norton, 1979.

Gilligan, Carol. *In a Different Voice: Psychological Theory and Women's Development*. Cambridge, MA: Harvard University Press, 1982.

Gray, Helen T. "Soul-Searching Survey." *Knight Ridder Newspapers*, February 15, 2003. http://www.religionnewsblog.com/2383/soul-searching-survey.

Holcomb, Justin S., and Lindsey A. Holcomb. *Is It My Fault? Hope and Healing for Those Suffering Domestic Violence.* Chicago: Moody, 2014.

Katz, Emily Tess, "Vocal Fry, Made Famous by Kim Kardashian, Is Making Young Women 'Less Hirable.'" *The Huffington Post*, November 3, 2014. http://www.huffingtonpost.com/2014/10/31/vocal-fry_n_6082220.html.

Kell, John. "Lean Times for the Diet Industry." *Fortune*. May 22, 2015. http://fortune.com/2015/05/22/lean-times-for-the-diet-industry/.

Kim, Eunjoo Mary. *Women Preaching: Theology and Practice through the Ages.* Eugene, OR: Wipf and Stock, 2004.

Knight, Dudley. *Speaking with Skill: An Introduction to Knight-Thompson Speechwork.* London: Bloomsbury Methuen Drama, 2012.

Lamb, Sharon, and Lyn Mikel Brown. *Packaging Girlhood: Rescuing Our Daughters from Marketers' Schemes.* New York: St. Martin's Press, 2006.

Lambroso, Daniel, and Olga Khazan. "The Science behind Hating Hillary Clinton's Voice." *The Atlantic*. Video. August 1, 2016.

Langberg, Diane Mandt. *Counseling Survivors of Sexual Abuse.* Wheaton, IL: Tyndale, 1997.

Lee, Charlotte I. *Oral Interpretation.* 4th ed. Boston: Houghton Mifflin, 1971.

Lee, Inn Sook, and Timothy D. Son, eds. *Asian Americans and Christian Ministry.* Seoul: Voice Publishing, 1999.

Lee, Won-Kyu. *Honorifics and Politeness in Korean.* Ann Arbor, MI: University Microfilm International; Dissertation Information Service, 1993.

Lerner, Harriet. *The Dance of Anger: A Woman's Guide to Changing the Patterns of Intimate Relationships.* New York: Quill, 2001.

————. *The Dance of Deception: A Guide to Authenticity and Truth-Telling in Women's Relationships.* New York: Quill, 2001.

Lewis, Karoline. John. Fortress Biblical Preaching Commentaries. Minneapolis: Fortress, 2014.

Liberman, Mark. "Uptalk Is Not HRT." *Language Log*, March 28, 2006. http://itre.cis.upenn.edu/~myl/languagelog/archives/002967.html.

Linklater, Kristin. *Freeing the Natural Voice.* Hollywood, CA: Drama Publishers, 2006.

Lowry, Gene L. *How to Preach a Parable: Designs for Narrative Sermons.* Nashville: Abingdon, 1989.

Maine, Margo, and Joe Kelly. *Body Myth: Adult Women and the Pressure to Be Perfect.* Hoboken, NJ: John Wiley, 2005.

————. *Body Wars: Making Peace with Women's Bodies.* Carlsbad, CA: Gürze Books, 2000.

Nam, Vickie, ed. *Yell-Oh Girls! Emerging Voices Explore Culture, Identity, and Growing Up Asian American.* New York: Quill, 2001.

National Coalition against Domestic Violence (NCADV). "Domestic Violence National Statistics." Accessed July 27, 2016. http://www.ncadv.org /files/National%20Statistics%20Domestic%20Violence%20NCADV.pdf.

National Sexual Violence Resource Center. "Statistics about Sexual Violence." 2015. http://www.nsvrc.org/sites/default/files/publications_nsvrc _factsheet_media-packet_statistics-about-sexual-violence_0.pdf.

Nichter, Mimi. *Fat Talk: What Girls and Their Parents Say about Dieting*. Cambridge, MA: Harvard University Press, 2000.

Nichter, Mimi, and Nancy Vukovic. "Fat Talk." In *Many Mirrors: Body Image and Social Relations*, edited by N. Sault, 109–31. New Brunswick, NJ: Rutgers University Press, 1994.

Nordquist, Richard. "Uptalk (high-rising terminal)," about education, November 27, 2015. http://grammar.about.com/od/tz/g/uptalkterm.htm.

Northrup, Christiane. *Women's Bodies, Women's Wisdom: Creating Physical and Emotional Health and Healing*. New York: Bantam, 2002.

Ogden, Cynthia L., Margaret D. Carroll, Brian K. Kit, and Katherine M. Flegal. "Prevalence of Childhood and Adult Obesity in the United States, 2011–2012." *Journal of the American Medical Association* 311, no. 8 (February 26, 2014). http://jama.jamanetwork.com/article.aspx?articleid=1832542.

"Old Fashioned Weight Loss Ads." *The Huffington Post*, March 2012. http://www .huffingtonpost.com/2012/03/25/vintage-weight-loss-ads_n_1373856 .html#gallery/216538/9.

Open Octave, "The Composer's Toolbox." Accessed August 7, 2016. http:// www.openoctave.org/the_composers_toolbox/orchestral_instruments /choir/soprano.

"Perform." Online Etymology Dictionary. Accessed June 28, 2016. http://www .etymonline.com/index.php?allowed_in_frame=0&search=perform.

Pipher, Mary. *Reviving Ophelia: Saving the Selves of Adolescent Girls*. New York: Ballantine, 1994.

Quinn, Janet F. *I Am a Woman Finding My Voice: Celebrating the Extraordinary Blessings of Being a Woman*. New York: Eagle Brook, 1999.

Rape, Abuse and Incest National Network (RAINN). "Perpetrators of Sexual Violence: Statistics." Accessed July 27, 2016. https://www.rainn.org /statistics/perpetrators-sexual-violence.

Sagalyn, Daniel. "Army General Calls for Changing Name of PTSD." PBS *Newshour*, November 4, 2011. http://www.pbs.org/newshour/updates /military-july-dec11-stress_11-04/.

Sandberg, Sheryl, and Adam Grant. "Speaking While Female: Why Women Stay Quiet at Work." *New York Times Sunday Review*, January 12, 2015. http:// www.nytimes.com/2015/01/11/opinion/sunday/speaking-while-female .html?_r=1.

Sataloff, Robert Thayer. *Professional Voice: The Science and Art of Clinical Care*. New York: Raven Press, 1991.

Shandler, Sara. *Ophelia Speaks: Adolescent Girls Write about Their Search for Self*. New York: Harper Perennial, 1999.

Shooter, Susan. *How Survivors of Abuse Relate to God: The Authentic Spirituality of the Annihilated Soul*. Surrey, UK: Ashgate, 2012.

Sichel, Deborah, and Jeanne Watson Driscoll. *Women's Moods: What Every Woman Must Know about Hormones, the Brain, and Emotional Health*. New York: William Morrow, 1999.

Simmons, Rachel. *Odd Girl Out, Revised and Updated: The Hidden Culture of Aggression in Girls*. New York: Mariner Books, 2011.

Simpson, C. Blake. "General Voice Care/Vocal Hygiene." UT Health Science Center (1996). http://uthscsa.edu/oto/voice.asp.

Theodorou, Angelina E. "Americans Are in the Middle of the Pack Globally When It Comes to Importance of Religion." Pew Research Center, December 23, 2015. http://www.pewresearch.org/fact-tank/2015/12/23/americans-are-in-the-middle-of-the-pack-globally-when-it-comes-to-importance-of-religion/.

Trible, Phyllis. "Bringing Miriam Out of the Shadows." *Bible Review* 5, no. 1 (February 1989): 14–25, 34.

Turner, Mary Donovan, and Mary Lin Hudson. *Saved from Silence: Finding Women's Voice in Preaching*. St. Louis: Chalice Press, 1999.

University of Iowa Voice-Academy. "Male and Female Voices." Accessed August 7, 2016. https://uiowa.edu/voice-academy/male-female-voices.

"Voice Feminization." Center for the Care of the Professional Voice. Accessed August 12, 2016. http://professionalvoice.org/feminization.aspx.

Webb, Stephen H. *The Divine Voice: Christian Proclamation and the Theology of Sound*. Grand Rapids: Brazos, 2004.

Weems, Renita J. *Just a Sister Away: A Womanist Vision of Women's Relationship in the Bible*. Philadelphia: Innisfree Press, 1988.

Women of Color in Ministry (WOCM) Project. Accessed June 19, 2016. http://womenofcolorinministry.org/index.html/.

Index of Names and Subjects

Index of Scripture References